Perceptions

A language is not a medium for messages but an organ of perception; collective, corporate perception. The discovery that languages are not channels like the telegraph, but basically forms of perception and association by perception, has been a tremendous revolution.
— *Marshall McLuhan*

STRATEGY ONE

Marketing means communicating your message. A communication is not what you say, but what is heard — and remembered. You influence the perception of a message by determining *how* it is expressed.

Remember when you experienced the frustration of talking to a friend or family member, only to discover later that they had completely misunderstood you? You knew what you said to them, but you didn't know what they heard, believed, assumed, or remembered. Then when you discovered the misunderstanding you had to spend even more time sorting out the mess. That little miscommunication may have cost you an opportunity, money, and time — not to mention some bad feelings.

> When a message is sent, and the receiver
> does not understand, who needs to change?
> The sender!

If you have communication problems with family and friends who know you and care about you, imagine the misunderstandings you will have with strangers. This chapter will give you many ideas and techniques for sending messages to the marketplace — but always from the point of view of how they are received and deciphered. Remember that. You must feel good about what you do. But it is more important that your clients and prospects feel good about what you do.

1.1 BELIEF

> Whether you believe you can or can not — you are right.
> — *HENRY FORD*

We make decisions based more on what we feel than on what we know, whether we are choosing a career, a life partner, friends, or products.

Some people are more analytical than others. They create a spreadsheet to decide which car or TV to buy. But after the spreadsheets have been examined, even the dedicated analyticals make decisions based on how they feel. After they make their decision they have to feel good about it. They may have to defend the choice to others, or to themselves. Sometimes they feel they've paid too much, but more often they feel they bought too cheap.

Power Marketing will show you how to influence the beliefs that help your customers buy you. Yes, buy *you*. Even though you are selling a service or product, first you have to get the prospect to buy you. Then they'll buy your service and products.

Our beliefs come from a mixture of our environment, experiences, knowledge, and emotions.

Our first beliefs tend to be strongest. Once entrenched, they are strengthened by more input that arrives through our senses — from what we see, hear, smell, touch, and taste. But all these inputs are filtered through our existing beliefs. If you can affect your customers' beliefs, you can affect their decisions.

Beliefs are powerful — they define us. Power Marketing is a way to affect customers' beliefs about you, your company, your product, and your industry.

> I wouldn't have seen it if I hadn't believed it.
> — *MARSHALL MCLUHAN*

Beliefs can be so powerful that they can prevent us from seeing what we do not understand or do not want to see. With Power Marketing, you will convey clear, conscious messages that your prospects will appreciate. But that is not enough. There are always unintended messages that accompany your conscious communications. You must become aware of the unintended messages you are sending and shape them to your cause.

Their belief system mixes, filters, and interprets messages.

1.2 IMAGE

In business, perception is reality.

Like many people, you may associate the word "image" with something that is phony or contrived. Instead, realize that "image" is the root for "imagine" — a powerful word. Imagine how you want to be, how you want to be seen, respected, and remembered.

THE POWER OF PRESENTATION

The president of an oil company remembers going shopping with his dad for a new car when he was a young boy. His father's business had done well and they were going to buy a brand new Cadillac. They entered the showroom, both of them proud and excited. They smiled as the salesman approached them. Then a strange thing happened. As the expectant salesman got closer, the smile on the father's face disappeared, and he reached down, grabbed his son's hand, turned around, and marched out. The boy was almost in tears. "What happened, Dad? Why did we leave?" His father barked, "I'll not buy an expensive car from a man with a soiled shirt." It seems the negligent salesman had worn his shirt two days in a row.

YOUR PERSONAL IMAGE

Think of yourself as a product with a brand image. How do you stand out from all the other products on the shelf? By creating and promoting Brand *You*! Consider what you want to be known for, and build those features into your brand design.

> I usually make up my mind about a man in ten seconds,
> and I very rarely change it.
> — MARGARET THATCHER

FIRST IMPRESSIONS

Strong beliefs are built on first impressions. We change our minds — but not easily. Your job is to make the first impression a good one.

First impressions both affect, and are affected by, our beliefs. When I see you for the first time, my beliefs about how someone in your business should look or act filter my opinion of you. A previous bad experience with someone from your industry will negatively colour how others see you. You will be judged by how you look, sound, and make them feel.

> We are what we repeatedly do.
> Excellence, then, is not an act, but a habit.
> — ARISTOTLE

Excellence is a habit

SELL YOURSELF

When you are the business and the only thing you offer is your service, it may be obvious that what you sell is yourself. But even if you sell goods for someone else's company, you sell yourself first, then your company, then your product. You are your greatest asset. Use that asset as your greatest marketing tool.

WATCH HOW YOU DRESS

You're probably thinking, "Not another pitch about dressing for success!" But even on casual Fridays you are judged by how you look. There is nothing wrong with dressing in casual clothing, if it is consistent with the message you want to send. Think about how your best client would expect you to look the first time they met you. Then remember that every time is a first time. Like it or not, you are being judged. Do you want your current clients to tell your prospects, "Yeah, I know he dresses poorly, but he's good — trust me"?

Dress like the professional you want them to believe you are. You might visit an image consultant for more advice. Explain the business you're in and how you want to be perceived by your clients and prospects. You can look different at the ball game and when you go out on Saturday night, but when on business, dress for business.

SMILE

The number one thing you can do to sell yourself is to smile more. Smile when you greet your clients. Smile when you enter their place. Smile at the receptionist when you ask to meet your contact. Smile when you say your name. Smile when they give you the order. Smile even when you do not get the business. (That's a tough one, but it's important.) Smile when they are talking. Smile when you describe your services. Smile — don't look guilty — when you tell them your price. Smile when you are on the phone. Smile when they hand you the payment — don't leer, just smile.

A smile conveys confidence in yourself, your product, and your company. A smile builds trust. We would rather do business with a face that smiles than one that frowns. When I line up at the grocery store, I will go to the checkout with the friendly cashier, even if it has the longest lineup.

In the global marketplace, a smile is the one gesture that is understood in any language, in any culture. And smiles are infectious. When you smile, others will smile back at you. Try it; it's hard to resist. When you smile, your brain releases endorphins that make you feel good. Imagine that — every time you smile, you make yourself and others feel better.

A man who opens a shop must learn to smile.

— *JEWISH PROVERB*

STAND AND WALK CONFIDENTLY

Body language sends hidden messages about how we feel. Others pick up on these signals unconsciously, and use them to make decisions about you. If you slouch and drag your feet, they assume you do not believe in yourself and your product. Whatever your shape, stand and walk your tallest and proudest. There's no need to strut like a peacock, of course; just look confident, even when you don't feel that way.

YOUR BRIEFCASE AND PEN

Replace your briefcase before it looks worn. You want to prevent prospects from thinking, "Gee, she can't even afford a new briefcase, I guess business must be bad." And when you open it — no surprises. Keep it neat and carry only what you need for that visit. Leave the rest (especially your sandwiches) back in the car or office. Your briefcase should project the image of the success you wish to be.

Don't carry a $0.19 plastic pen to business meetings. When you go out, look the part, right down to your pen. You don't have to invest $50 or $100 on a pen, just get one that looks expensive. Then watch for the nod of approval when you offer it to the client who's about to sign the agreement.

YOUR HEALTH

Longer life and more enjoyment are only two of the obvious reasons to have good health. In business, your health sends messages about you. Take care of yourself, and you'll be seen as a well-disciplined and forward-thinking person. You don't have to run marathons, but keep in mind that many deals are made on the golf links or at the fitness club.

SHAKING HANDS

You make an impression when you shake hands. Use a firm handshake while looking your contact in the eye. The acceptable handshake duration varies around the world. In North America, a good rule is to shake until you can identify the colour of the other person's eyes. In northern Europe, the handshake is short. In Latin cultures, be prepared to share a long and enthusiastic handshake — maybe even a hug. In Japan, you bow. Wherever you meet people, show interest and delight while greeting and listening to them.

Be aware of the dominant and submissive handshakes. In a handshake between two "equals," the hands are side by side, with neither dominating. An individual who feels superior to you will extend his or her hand with the palm down, taking the superior position and thus dominating you. This person does not see you as an equal in your partnership. On the other hand, the person who automatically holds their hand palm up feels inferior to you. There is an opportunity to help this person.

INTRODUCING YOURSELF

You may have heard your name thousands of times, so to save time you state it very quickly. The listener does not hear your name and won't remember you. Say your name slowly and clearly so they hear it. Enunciate for them. "Hi, I am (short pause) George (longer pause) Torok (pause and smile)." Look happy to state your name. If you have a difficult or unusual name, repeat it. You might help them remember it by saying, "rhymes with . . ." or "in my mother tongue it means . . ." And if you can make people laugh when you say your name, they will remember you.

State your name clearly when meeting face to face, talking on the phone, or introducing yourself to a group. Be proud of your name and show it. Never apologize for introducing yourself.

> If I dyed my hair, they'd want more speed.
> — GORDIE HOWE AT AGE FIFTY-FIVE

PHOTOGRAPHS

When you use your picture on flyers, cards, or stationery, get it professionally done. But don't change your appearance so much that clients don't recognize you when they meet you.

STRATEGIC PHOTOGRAPHY

Have you ever seen someone's photo in a brochure or article and then later met them in person? Did they look the same, or were they ten or twenty years older than their photo?

I believe it's better to hear someone say, "You look so much younger than your picture, Mr. Bender," than it is to hear, "You look much older than I expected!" To accomplish the former, I used to sprinkle powder in my hair before having photos taken, to emphasize the grey. I can use those pictures for many years and they still look current.

(I've also discovered that professional photographers can now do the same thing using computer software. It looks great, and it's a lot easier than powder!)

— PETER

LEARNING AND LISTENING

By reading this book you are showing you are willing to learn. Let that willingness to learn show through in how you approach your business. Most want to deal with experts, but no one wants to do business with a know-it-all.

Show a willingness to listen to clients and learn. Ask your prospects probing questions, and listen carefully to their responses. Show that you are committed to learning and improving your knowledge and skills by taking courses, attending seminars, and reading. Mention these endeavours in your conversations so your clients know you are good and getting better — in order to serve them better. When you mention lessons from seminars, books, and life, sprinkle lightly like spice; don't smear it on like peanut butter.

> What you do speaks so loudly
> that I cannot hear what you say.
> — RALPH WALDO EMERSON

Your Company Image: Vision, Mission, Slogan, and Purpose

What is the difference between a company's vision, mission statement, slogan, and purpose statement? Many get them confused. And it's no wonder. Not so long ago, corporations became convinced by the consulting industry that every company needed these types of statements. Consultants rushed in, claiming to be "mission statement experts" and voilà! Soon there was a mish-mash of multi-page statements that confused and created more cynicism among staff and clients of the corporations. It became difficult to tell one type of statement from another.

Don't get me wrong. Vision, mission, slogan, and purpose are important concepts that can help you guide your business. But there's no reason you can't develop them yourself. To get you started, here is a brief overview of what the terms mean. I expect that a consultant would use ten times as many words to explain them — and of course they charge by the word.

Note that writing these statements will require some serious thinking and wordsmithing on your part, but the work will pay off when your customers buy in to your approach — and buy your product.

Vision is a big-picture statement. To find your vision you ask yourself "Why?" Your vision must be powerful, summarized in one memorable or motivating sentence or phrase. It should be general in scope, not restricting. Because "why?" is so powerful a question, the answer is almost spiritual.

Truly good corporate vision statements are few and far between. My favourite vision statement is the one for the *Star Trek* series of television shows and movies:

"Space. The Final Frontier." Repeat that aloud as you gaze up at the starry night sky. Feel the power in that statement.

The *mission statement* is nearly as big and powerful as the vision. To discover your mission, ask the question, "What am I going to do about my vision?" This statement must also be short — one sentence or phrase, not paragraphs! It must be equally memorable and motivating. It is more general than specific.

Following on the *Star Trek* theme, the mission there is "to seek out new life, to go where no one has gone before."

Notice how short, simple, and powerful that is. And think about how long this famous statement has been around (and how many times it has been recited by fans of the shows). By contrast, the lengthy, weasel-worded proclamations that corporations have spent so much time and money on tend to be quickly forgotten or abandoned.

Your *purpose statement* is very specific compared to the other statements. It is the best answer to give when a prospect asks, "What do you do?" More about this below.

A *slogan* is a phrase you use like a logo. It doesn't necessarily mention your product or service. It may describe a feeling, the way you work, or your strength. Every time it is heard you want people to think of you.

YOUR VISION AND MISSION

Invest the time to think about the vision and mission for your business. It's important not to overlook this very fundamental step to success. And don't make the common mistake of thinking your mission is to make money. That would certainly be one of your goals but not your mission. Your mission statement is supposed to make your customer want to do business with you. If you tell him or her, "My mission is to make a lot of money," don't be surprised if they slam the door in your face. Making a profit is no more the raison d'être for your business than eating food is for living. But you need to eat food to live and you need to make a profit to maintain your business.

An executive at John Deere, one of the world's oldest farm machinery companies, told me that her company is in the business of "helping farmers feed the world." That is a noble mission and one that people can relate to. Sure, their main product is farm machinery, but that is the detail, not the mission. Many manufacturers of farm machinery have come and gone. John Deere is long-lived because it knows its mission *and* it makes a profit.

Make your mission statement a noble one — one that helps your customers want to do business with you.

He that is of the opinion money will do everything
may well be suspected of doing everything for money.
— *BENJAMIN FRANKLIN*

When Masaru Ibuka and Akito Morita established the Tokyo Tsushin
Kogyo company after the end of WWII, the first thing they did was
write down the company's philosophy. Its initial products — radio
parts and a rice cooker — didn't last, but Sony's philosophy did.

YOUR PURPOSE STATEMENT

Think long and hard about what it is that you do, in practical terms, and
write it down concisely.

Here is my purpose statement: I specialize in helping corporate managers and small business owners present themselves with more confidence
and impact. I also work with sales and marketing people to improve the
effectiveness of their sales presentations.

The key components are as follows:

"I specialize"	Be a specialist, not a generalist.
"in helping"	Do not overpromise. You help, not guarantee.
"corporate managers and small business owners"	Identify your prime market.
"present themselves with more confidence and impact"	Indicate the change you bring.
"I also work with sales and marketing"	Acknowledge your secondary market.
"to improve the effectiveness of their sales presentations"	Identify a secondary benefit.

If your purpose statement is well written your prospect should be prompted
to say, "That's interesting. How do you do that?" Then you go into more
detail. Notice that this statement should take less than fifteen seconds to
read or say. If it is powerful and they are interested, you will get more of
their time. Tell me you can't hold someone's attention for fifteen seconds.

YOUR SLOGAN

A slogan is often used in advertising campaigns. An effective slogan is one that customers remember (or even hum!) and associate with the company.

Some effective slogans

Nothing runs like a Deere.	John Deere	farm machinery
Coke Is It / The Real Thing / Catch the Wave	Coca-Cola	soft drink
Our product is steel. Our strength is people.	Dofasco	steel manufacturer
At Speedy you're a somebody.	Speedy Muffler King	muffler shop
Harvey's makes a hamburger a beautiful thing.	Harvey's Restaurants	fast food
From sharp minds come Sharp products.	Sharp Electronics	electronics
If it's on time, it's a Fluke.	Fluke Transport	trucking
We care about the shape you're in.	Wonderbra	bras
Will that be cash or Chargex?	Chargex (Visa)	credit card

Now create your own slogan. Write words that describe some aspect of your product or service. How do you want your customers to feel after they buy? Your slogan could even take the form of a question. Keep it short — no more than seven words. You will need to play with various combinations. Try it out on some colleagues first, then on a few customers.

Often more is less. In 1892 Henry Heinz was searching for a company slogan. He settled on "57 varieties" to describe the company's foods. In fact, they had sixty products, but "57" sounds like more and it had a better ring. It has survived the test of time.

YOUR COMPANY NAME

It can be tough to choose your company name. If you are providing a service and you are a one-person firm, use your own name in the company name. Make it easy for your customers to remember you. Give them one thing to remember rather than two.

If I were to start over I might name my company "Peter Urs Bender — Power Presentations"; George might name his "George Torok Seminars." These say what we do and are easy to remember. Compare them with the names we did choose: "The Achievement Group" and "The Knowledge Navigators." Both are impressive names — but is it clear what business we are in?

Stay away from "Clark Kent and Associates." Instead consider . . .

Clark Kent The Superman
Clark Kent Rescues
Clark Kent Hero-on-Call
Clark Kent Man of Steel
Clark Kent Adventures

But do not overstate the nature of your company! For example, names like

Peter Urs Bender University
George Torok Institute
Lee Smith Global Enterprises

tend to be too much and may diminish your credibility.

In 1924 Thomas Watson Sr. changed the name of the Computing-Tabulating-Recording Company to International Business Machines. The company had no international operations at that time but they had vision.

What's in a name?

Choosing a product or company name is more critical when your business operates in other cultures and languages. It could be mildly embarrassing or disastrous if you make a mistake.

International marketing ideas that *didn't* work!

1. Coors translated its slogan "Turn it loose" into Spanish. Unfortunately, in that language it was read as "Suffer from diarrhea."
2. Scandinavian vacuum manufacturer Electrolux used the following in an American campaign: "Nothing sucks like an Electrolux."
3. Clairol introduced their "Mist Stick" curling iron into Germany, only to find out that "mist" is slang for manure. Not too many people had use for a "manure stick."
4. When Gerber started selling baby food in Africa, they used the same packaging as in the U.S., with a beautiful Caucasian baby on the label. Later they learned that in Africa, since many could not read at that time, companies routinely labelled bottles with pictures of what's inside.
5. Colgate introduced a toothpaste in France called Cue, the name of a notorious porno magazine.
6. An American T-shirt maker in Miami printed shirts for the Spanish market to promote the Pope's visit. Instead of "I saw the Pope" (*el Papa*), the shirts read, "I saw the potato" (*la papa*).
7. Pepsi's "Come alive with the Pepsi generation" translated into Chinese as "Pepsi brings your ancestors back from the grave."
8. Frank Perdue's chicken slogan, "It takes a strong man to make a tender chicken," was translated into Spanish as "It takes an aroused man to make a chicken affectionate."
9. The Coca-Cola name in China was first read as *ke-kou-ke-la*, meaning "bite the wax tadpole" or "female horse stuffed with wax," depending on the dialect. Coke then researched 40,000 characters to find a phonetic equivalent *ko-kou-ko-le*, which translates to "happiness in the mouth."
10. When Parker Pen marketed a ballpoint pen in Mexico, its ads were supposed to have read, "It will not leak in your pocket and embarrass you." Instead, the company thought that the word *embarazar* (to impregnate) meant to embarrass, so the ad read, "It will not leak in your pocket and make you pregnant."

Walt Disney took the advice of his wife, Lillian, and named his cartoon mouse Mickey instead of his first choice — Mortimer.

BUSINESS CARDS

You must have business cards. Keep them simple. Print large enough for most to read. It is annoying to have to strain your eyes while reading someone's card. Might any of your prospects have failing eyesight? If they are baby boomers, they probably do. Do you want the first impression to annoy them?

Less is more. Print your name, address, phone number, fax number, e-mail number, web address, logo, and slogan. Your card is your first line of marketing. It tells people what you do and how to reach you.

Make people want to keep your card. Put something of value on the back, such as a calendar, quotation, poker hands, or tips.

When you give someone your business card, present it. Treat it with respect. Don't just toss it on the table. The Japanese make a ceremony out of trading business cards. You don't have to perform this ceremony in western culture, but if you present your card with a little flair, most will notice the value and respect you convey.

Always carry your business cards with you and give them out. But remember that it's far more important to get business cards than it is to hand them out. Then you can control the contact. Whenever someone asks for your card, be sure to ask for theirs. When you receive their card look at it with interest, read it (if the print is large enough), and repeat the person's name and company name out loud. They will be delighted that you read it. Comment on their logo or mission statement.

When you receive a business card, write on the back of the card any information that is important for you to remember about this person: important dates, their level of interest, where you met them, and so on. Some networking experts will tell you that it is rude to write on people's cards right in front of them. This is true according to Asian custom. You can get by this obstacle by querying, "Do you mind if I write that on your card so I do not forget?" Design your own coding system. Use numbers, letters, checkmarks, stars, and symbols that tell you what to do with this contact when you return to your office. Make it simple so you can make a quick note and understand it later.

Sample Coding System

A hot prospect
B interested but nothing now
C no interest but follow up
1 call tomorrow
2 send information
* ask for a date
$ discussed price

When collecting cards at a meeting you will often get cards you have no intention of keeping. Don't waste time; accept the card and put it in your left pocket. The keepers go in your right pocket. It doesn't matter which pockets you use, as long as you have a system.

Business cards are fundamental marketing tools. Don't leave home without them.

LOGO

Should you have a logo? An effective logo can be a great identifier because most people remember images better than names. A logo can stand out in a sea of words, especially if it is simple, unique, and memorable.

If you are very good with graphics you might design your own. Otherwise, hire a graphic artist. You don't have to spend a lot of money. You can find talented and inexpensive artists through your local college or university.

When designing a logo, keep the following features in mind. Your logo should be:

- Timeless. Technology moves rapidly. Avoid using images such as a steam locomotive, an Apollo space capsule, or bell-bottomed trousers.
- Simple and recognizable. You don't want your customers staring at your logo as if they were trying to understand a Picasso. The design should work well both in black and white and in colour.
- Unique. You want it to stand out. And you don't want your company mistaken for another.
- Compatible. It should fit your company or your mission.

When you have a logo, use the colour version on your web site and your stationery. Use a simpler, text-only version on your e-mail signature, discussion group signature, or e-mail brochures. Use the logo on all your messages so it becomes associated with your company.

STATIONERY

Will you get any business because you have nice stationery? No. But you may lose business if you do not. It is so much easier for prospects to say no when your correspondence looks cheap or unprofessional, especially when you are a new company.

Invest in stationery that projects the image you need. You could visit an office supply store and get something "off the rack." But remember, that says you're an "off-the-rack" business — one of many.

Have a custom look designed for you. Hire a graphic designer to create a look that links your business cards, stationery, and flyers. Pick a paper that looks and feels right.

If you do a lot of faxing, test the paper. Flecked paper looks dirty on the receiving end. Embossing doesn't even show through the fax. Some colours fax better than others. Reds do not fax or photocopy well. You could also design special "for fax" stationery.

Always print more than you think you need. Once it's printed you will find more uses for it than you ever expected. And the unit cost drops significantly for higher print runs. Ask your printer about the quantity price breaks.

Colours

Colours influence emotion. Think about the emotion you want to convey and test your choices on several members of your target group before you make your final selection. Talk with your graphic designer. Hot pinks get noticed, but do you want your business associated with hot pinks? Blues are generally a good business colour, but not all blues will work. Reds are not a good colour to use if you are selling to accountants, because it reminds them of losses. Maintain a consistent colour and layout through all your materials. Too many colours detract from your message. Keep to no more than two colours plus white.

When choosing colours, think about what colour of paper you will use. Blue ink turns green on yellow paper; red turns purple on blue; purple ink turns black on green; most colours (except white) disappear on black.

Imagine how sharp your signature will look when you sign in the same colour ink used to print your letterhead (assuming you use a colour other than plain black). Ask your printer the *pantone number* of the ink on your stationery. Then buy a pen of that colour from an art supply store. This tip is courtesy of Donald Cooper, a professional speaker specializing in marketing and service innovation. He uses the pen to handwrite short notes on his letters. It looks great!

Notepaper

Print your notepaper in the same pattern as your letterhead, but on 4" x 6" or 5 1/2" x 8 1/2" paper. Often notepaper is far more useful than letterhead. For one thing, you and your client both save time if you send a short handwritten note, because they're easier to compose and faster to read. And you connect more effectively when your notes are personalized.

Envelopes

Print your name big and bold on the outside of your envelopes. Don't be mysterious about who they're from. If you include your logo and marketing message on the outside, everyone who sees the envelope receives your message. If you think the only way they will open your mail is if they don't know it's from you, then they're not likely to read it when they do open it. And they will be annoyed at you.

Post-it notes

These are great — even better than notepaper. Write short notes on them and stick them on articles, flyers, etc. We read post-it notes first because they attract our attention. They are personal because you handwrite them and address them to the person you're trying to contact. Post-it notes come in many colours but I still prefer the original yellow. They're likely to stand out from the paper they're stuck to, and don't assault the eyes like the hot neon colours do.

mail / Follow up to ensure received it

Custom-printed post-it notes

Go one better. Have your name and phone number printed on post-it notes. You can include your slogan or product name. I have several versions printed with different product names. They are a little expensive but they are unique. In fact, one of the reasons I decided to go with them is *because* they are expensive. It meant my competition was less likely to get them. To reduce my unit cost I ordered tons. They will last me years.

MAIL AND FREIGHT

Identify your shipping needs. Then do a little research and establish accounts before you have to ship something. That way when the need arises you can avoid last-minute panic.

It's always a good idea to get to know your couriers and post-office representatives. Show them the type of mail and packages you typically send out. Ask about their rates, their drop-off times, and how long they take for delivery. Know the location and pick-up times of the nearest mailboxes so you can drop your mail each day.

In Canada, use "Express Post envelopes." Buy them from your post office in three sizes. Because they are prepaid, they are very convenient. Just put your material in them and drop them in the nearest mailbox. Make sure you drop Express Post envelopes in a box that is cleared the same day.

Express Post envelopes cost more than regular mail but are cheaper than most courier services. They arrive faster than regular mail (they're generally guaranteed for the next day), they send a message that you value time, and they stand out in the mail pile. If you buy them in bulk you will get a discounted rate. Because they are prepaid you can stuff as much in as will fit.

> When you need information to make a decision
> you want it quickly.

There is nothing like the impression a client gets when you talk to them today, and they receive your package the very next day! A few days after you know it should have arrived, call your client to confirm that the package or information was received. They will be impressed with the fast delivery and then with your follow-up.

PHONES

Your phone and how you use it tells a lot about you.

> Mr. Watson, come in here. I need you.
> — *THE FIRST PHONE CALL FROM ALEXANDER GRAHAM BELL*

Outgoing calls

Chapter 5, on maintaining a database, contains tips on cold calling and other outgoing calls. But your outgoing calls can have a great impact on your image and how customers perceive you, so here are some words of advice.

When talking to clients, focus on the conversation at hand. Listen to their words and tone.

Do not try to do other jobs at the same time. You will only do both poorly. On the other hand, when you're chatting with friends during business hours, do other jobs at the same time. Let them know how busy you are.

Sit up straight. You'll sound better. Or stand — you'll sound even better. Most of us think better on our feet. And you will tend to make shorter calls if standing.

When you're on the phone, sit or stand the way you would if the other person were across from you in your office. Animate your conversation as if they were there. Nod and gesture. Don't slouch. Place a mirror where you use the phone so you can check your posture and smile. Yes, smile — even when talking on the phone. Smiling makes you sound friendly and confident. Smiling makes you feel good, even when your customer says no. Smiling keeps you from getting angry.

Keep calls to three minutes or less. If you call your client ten times for three minutes each they will remember you more than if you call them once for thirty minutes.

Most of the time it is better to talk to twenty prospects for three minutes each than it is to call two for thirty minutes each. Note, both strategies use sixty minutes of your time but the first is likely to be more effective.

Incoming calls

What does your phone say about you? If you operate your business from home, have a separate line for business. Make your message sound professional. Your children are cute — but record your own business voice message.

Here are some of the biggest errors people make when recording their greeting for incoming calls:

- Failing to identify the company. ("You have reached 555-5555" may be okay for your personal line, but not for business.)
- Having a long message without telling callers how to skip the message. (You may wish to tell the caller to press the "pound" [#] or "star" [*] key to get directly to your voice mail.)
- Allowing the phone to ring more than twice before the answering service clicks on (or a human being picks up the phone).
- Recording a cutesy message, music, or sound effects. I know one guy who recorded the sound of a toilet flushing, so that callers could guess why he could not answer the phone.
- Saying "I might be on another line or I might be out." Who cares where you might be? This information is not helpful and wastes callers' time.
- Leaving a vague and impersonal message, such as "Someone will get back to you."
- Stating the date, and forgetting to change the message the next day. I've reached messages that are days old.

To avoid these and other problems, here are some tips that really work:

- Call your own phone to check how the message sounds and feels.
- Remove unnecessary words — shorter is better.
- Remove all negative words.
- Ask for feedback from friends.

- Drink water before you record your message.
- After you record your message, play it back, especially if you change your message often.
- If customers tend to call with common questions, set up a mailbox with a recording of the answers (e.g., "For directions on how to find our store, press 1. For tips on how to program your VCR, press 2. To order a copy of our book, press 3," and so on).
- After you record these messages, call back and check each one.
- Ask a friend to check your voice mail periodically and give you feedback. Reward them for their help.
- Set the answering machine or voice mail service to pick up after one ring when you are not there. This shows your customers that you respect their time.
- Tell callers you will get back to them within x number of hours; then do what you say.
- If you mention the date, change your message the night before. If you won't change the message every day, then do not make it date sensitive.

Leaving a voice message for your clients and prospects

Always state your name and number twice — once at the very beginning and again at the end of your message. If they need to replay the message they won't have to listen to it all the way through just to hear your phone number.

Here's a foolproof three-step process for leaving good voice messages:

1. State your name and number. When leaving your name, sound it out very clearly and s-l-o-w-l-y. It helps if you spell a tricky name. Or play the name game: "Sounds like . . ." P-l-e-a-s-e s-l-o-w d-o-w-n when leaving your phone number.
2. State the purpose of your call:

"I am returning your call about the Simpson contract. I will be in my office this afternoon looking forward to your call to discuss the details."

"I am following up on the information I sent you about my training programs on presentation skills. I look forward to setting up a training schedule for your managers. Call me when you have some dates in mind."

"Three things. One, I'm available for October 2. Two, we can meet next Tuesday at 3:00 to clarify your needs. Three, I will honour the fee schedule from the last project."

Don't blather. Make your messages clear and short.

3. Restate your name and number.
   Again, state both, slowly and clearly.

Always leave your phone number, even if you know they have it. It is courteous and it saves them from having to look it up. It may be that they are checking their voice mail from out of the office and don't have their list of phone numbers with them. If you leave your number they can call you before they get back to the office.

When leaving a voice message you can usually review it and erase and re-record if you do not like your first attempt. On my phone system you press the "pound" key to get these menu options. Try replaying your message the next time you get someone's voice mail, just to hear how you sound.

Sounding bigger is better

Are you a one-person show operating from your home? Would you like to appear larger than you are? Many still view home businesses as temporary. Others might think you are doing this until you get a real job.

Hello? I can't take your call right now because I'm cleaning my fish tank.

Here are some dieting tips to help you look bigger than you are:

- Affiliate with companies in other cities and countries — then list your national and international offices.
- Say "we."
- Never offer the fact that you are a "one-person operation," or that you operate from your home. It may come out later but do not mention it at the beginning of your relationship.
- Talk about being in the office, not in your home. Corporate people still don't fully trust the home entrepreneur.
- Keep the kids and dog away when you are on the phone.
- Arrange with friends or colleagues to use their corporate meeting rooms when you need one. Trade something for this, such as a product or service, a favour, or lunch.
- Do not tell your customer that you just got out of the shower.
- Do not tell them that you are in your sweats — or naked.
- Make mention of your team, which includes your accountant, your shipper, your printer, and so on. But don't invent anyone. Be truthful.
- Use the word "centre" or "group" in your company name.
- Have a separate phone line for your business. This is very important!
- Do not let your kids answer the business phone during business hours. And remember that business hours could be any hour of the day and night, including weekends.
- Record your phone message using the word "we."
- When you are away, arrange for a colleague to pick up your calls. Do the same for them.

It's okay to be a one-person show, but we still tend to associate success with size. Never be ashamed of your small operation — even Godzilla was a one-creature show.

Sometimes you might feel like Godzilla, with the whole world against you. The truth is, the whole world doesn't care about you. Like Godzilla, you have to thrash about and roar to be seen and heard.

Cell phones and car phones

It is extremely annoying when you are meeting with someone and their cell phone rings. It is even more aggravating if they answer it. They take the call while you sit there twiddling your thumbs. Don't do this to your clients.

No one has my cell number. I only use it to check my voice mail when I am out and to call clients if I am delayed on the way to meet with them. If you give someone your cell phone number, they can and will call you anywhere at the most inconvenient times. Instead, give them one number — your office number. Check your voice mail often when you're out. If you don't want to miss an important call, forward your office calls to your cell phone. That way you keep your cell number private.

Cell phones are no longer novelties. It doesn't impress people anymore if you have a cell phone. Get one if you need it. But they are not a badge of importance.

It shows respect for your clients when you turn off your cell phone and beeper when you meet with them. You can always check your messages right after the meeting. This seems like a simple rule but I still see some people breaking it.

> A little neglect may breed great mischief . . .
> for want of a nail the shoe was lost;
> for want of a shoe the horse was lost;
> and for want of a horse the rider was lost.
> — BENJAMIN FRANKLIN

YOUR CAR

Your car sends a message about how successful you are. Maintain it. A rusty car is never cool. If you have an old car, get it repainted. Customers might think that you are an antique collector. But if it is rusty they know you have no money. If you have no money they think you are not successful in your business. And if you are not successful you must not be good.

If you drive an old car, you might rent or borrow a better one for an important meeting.

Keep your car clean inside and out, even if — no, especially if — it is the family car. When you are on business it is okay to have a baby seat in the back, but not the diapers.

Advertise on the go (margin handwriting)

Use your car as a signboard. Paint your name on the sides if it fits the image of your business. If you're in a big city with tall buildings, put your name on the roof of the car. If signs are not appropriate, then you can always go with vanity plates.

> If it walks like a duck,
> and quacks like a duck,
> then it just may be a duck.
> — WALTER REUTHER

SUCCESS

Most people prefer to deal with successful companies.

If you want my business, don't come begging for it — show that you do not need it. There is more to looking successful than exuberantly answering, "I'm fantastic!" whenever someone asks, "How are you?"

Name drop. Mention other customers' names, especially if they're well known and respected. If you are doing business far away or internationally, let it be known.

If a well-known company like IBM is a satisfied customer (even if it was only one small job), we respect that more than hearing that the Mom & Pop restaurant has been happy with your service for ten years. We assume that IBM is more discerning. It's not necessarily true, but in business, perception is reality. That's why the big-name celebrities get those product endorsements. We all want to be like successful people and companies.

When answering questions from clients, throw in remarks like "When I was helping ABC Corporation with this same problem . . ." or "Last month when I was working for a client in Europe . . ." But only tell the truth. Never lie.

If you are travelling out of the country, mention that on your voice message. You sound important if someone wants you in other countries.

Celebrate milestones. Congratulate your tenth, one hundredth, or one thousandth customer. Have a party for your anniversary dates. Make it big and publicize it.

McDonald's signs used to proclaim "Over 1,000,000 sold." Now the sign reads "Billions and billions sold." Their products must be good if they sold so many.

A final note on success: Success breeds success, and winners like to hang out with winners. Make a point of meeting with other successful business owners. You will learn from them and see that it can be done.

Price is what you pay. Value is what you get.
— *WARREN BUFFETT*

1.3 VALUE

Not only must you provide value, but you must also show that you value your clients — their money, risk, time, staff, product, and needs.

Always underpromise and overdeliver.

Promise	*Deliver*
"I'll get it to you within one week."	Have it delivered in two days.
"It will cost about $1,000."	It costs $950.
"I will be at your office by noon."	You arrive at 11:45 a.m.
"I will need thirty minutes of your time."	You use twenty minutes.

Be known for keeping your promise — and then some.
Be honest. Never promise what you cannot deliver.

Value is not the same as cost. In fact, a product's value is almost never equal to its cost. For example, your product might cost you $2 and you sell it for $10. The value to you is $10. The value to the customer will usually be more than the selling price. If it was only worth $10 to the customer then they have no motivation to buy. But if the value to them is greater than the selling price, they are motivated to trade their money for something of greater value. It may be worth $30 to the customer. Then they will gladly give up $10 of their money for the product. The greater

↑ perceived value of the product → ↑ desire to purchase

the difference between the perceived value and the cost of the purchase, the more the customer will want to do business with you.

Always provide value that is greater than the price they pay.

THE VALUE FORMULA

Take a look at the following formula, then see where you need to concentrate your efforts to create value. Every product and service can be described this way.

Total value = real value + perceived value

Let's take it apart to understand it. *Real value* comprises the tangibles. It is relatively easy to measure. Real value can be expressed in this manner:

Real value = function/cost

Function is what the product or service does in mechanical or analytical terms. How much money does it save you or make for you?

Imagine you are buying a new car. If you want to get the best *real value*, you would get the most *function* — efficient ground transportation — for the lowest *cost*.

You could measure the car's *function* factor by comparing it with the cost of your practical alternatives — public transit, car pooling, taxi, bicycle, limousine, various car models. You might wish to consider the costs of these alternatives in terms of time and inconvenience. What does your new car give you that these other modes of transportation don't?

Having determined the new car's function factor, you can divide it by its cost. Is its function worth more to you than its cost? If so, the new car has *real value*.

At the end of your analysis you would buy the cheapest car. Right? Not necessarily. Remember that what you are willing to pay for your car is based on the *total value* to you, which is a factor of both *real* and *perceived* value. So, sometimes without realizing it, you assign value to less quantifiable benefits and buy something that you *like*. *Liking* is not part of real value — it is part of a product's *perceived value*.

Compared with real value, perceived value is harder to measure. It is influenced by emotion, image, and other intangibles —(all the benefits you should emphasize in your marketing efforts.) Perceived values

Perceived values are not bad — they are a reality. As long as we are individuals we will think differently, perceive differently, and place different values on things.

Be aware of that. Use it to your advantage. When your prospect wants to negotiate price, remember to build up your product's perceived value.

By the way, always deliver real value too.

ADDING VALUE

How do you provide more value to your customers? As we've seen, there are two types of value — real and perceived. Customers buy both, and most of the time they don't know the difference. You might point that difference out when your competitor is perceived to be superior. When you are perceived to be better, enhance that image.

COST

If you plan to be the low-cost producer, then be aware of the market you will attract. If you market yourself as top of the line, deliver what you promise.

Cost may be important to your customers, but if you focus only on cost, you deprive your customers of other value-added benefits in terms of time, image, and service.

QUALITY

What is quality? Buyers of Honda Civic, Ford Taurus, and Rolls-Royce all claim to buy quality. And they are all right. The secret of quality is to deliver what you promise. To delight your customers, meet their expectations, and deliver a little bit more.

When we speak of quality, we often confuse reality and perception. At one time buying IBM products was the smart decision to make, even if they were not the best. The name implied quality. Was that quality real or perceived?

Another way of understanding quality is by looking at the ISO 9000 certifications that are issued by the International Standards Organization. Because quality standards vary country by country, this type of certification is required for anyone operating in the global market. It can be applied to manufacturers, service providers, and even governments. But, curiously, this set of guidelines is not a quality standard in the traditional sense. To be certified, applicants must provide a detailed written description of their process. Then they must prove to the ISO auditors that they actually do what they say. They either pass or fail. Under this certification system, the three auto manufacturers listed above all meet the same "quality standard." In essence, they do what they say. And that is a great definition of quality.

You do not need to be ISO 9000 certified, but why not test your methods? Write down your processes, then test yourself. Do you do what you say?

TIME

The competitive advantage of the new millennium is time. This means respecting your customers' time. How long does it take for your customer to get through to you? How long do you take to respond? How long does it take them to fill out your silly paperwork? How long does it take to receive the product? How long does it take for you to upgrade and develop new products? Identify at least one area in which you beat your competition on time.

IMAGE

Your personal and company image can add to or detract from the perceived value of your product. Do you reach into your pocket for a cheap pen or a Mont Blanc? Do you arrive in a limo or a cab? Image is a strange thing. We might say it is not important, yet we find ourselves judging others on their image. Watch it! Your prospects are judging you. Why do we trust the millionaire basketball player who tells us which expensive running shoes to buy? When you are planning a joint promotion, what companies do you want to associate with your name? Who will enhance your image?

SERVICE

This is another term that is hard to define. Do you smile when you greet your customers, even on the phone? Are you easy to reach with a problem? How quickly do you respond to a problem and reach an acceptable solution? Do you make your customers feel inadequate when they complain, or do you welcome the feedback? After you sell the product, are you still interested in your customer, even if they only want information on how to use the product?

Today, companies are focusing on customer service like never before. Unfortunately, there are still frontiers to be discovered.

REVOLTING CUSTOMER SERVICE

Picture a boardroom. The sales manager announces, "The customers are revolting!" The president answers, "Yes, I know, but after a while you get used to them."

Here is my nomination for the Revolting Customer Service Award.

When I pay my charge card at the bank on a Friday, they have that annoying sign proclaiming, "Operating on Monday's date."

Me: "Hi, I'm here to pay my bill and I want it recorded on today's date."

The Bank (pointing to sign): "Oh, but I'm operating on Monday's date."

Me: "That is nice. I am operating on today's date."

The Bank (more indignant now): "Sir, I am operating on Monday's date."

Me: "I and the rest of the world are on today's date. Today is Friday, my bill is due today, and I am in the bank today. Please give me a receipt for today."

Sometimes they give me a handwritten receipt for the Friday, although they stamp my bill with Monday's date.

What if I had tried to withdraw money instead?

Me: "Hi, I want to withdraw $5,000 from my account."

The Bank: "But sir, there is only $100 in your account."

Me: "Yes, today there is only $100 in my account, but on Monday there will be $5,000 and I notice that you are operating on next day's date. So please give me $5,000 in cash today."

I walk across the plaza to another bank. I pay another bill. They accept the payment and date my receipt for Friday. That's customer service.

— *GEORGE*

How do you revolt your customers?
And what are you doing about it?

LISTENING

The best way to show clients that you value them is to listen to them. You learn information about them and their business. You discover their pain and passion — the secrets to meeting their needs. And they feel good about you, because you show interest in them! This is more powerful than most people think. Meeting customer needs involves listening to their needs — not deciding on your own what is best for them. By asking questions and listening, you will discover how to sell to them, you'll see other opportunities, and you'll be warned of impending dangers.

During the many years I spent buying and negotiating for millions of dollars for my employer, I was amazed and perplexed by the salespeople who were so intent on giving their presentation that they never took the time to listen. Sometimes I needed what they were selling, but whenever I had the discretion, out the door they went.

— *GEORGE*

If you put a small value on yourself,
rest assured that the world will not raise your price.

PRICING

Decide where you want to position yourself in the price market. Do you want to be the lowest priced, middle of the pack, or most expensive? Once you pick your position you will be stuck with it. Sure, you can raise your prices as you get better, but you are stuck with an image and position. Wal-Mart and Tiffany & Co. are positioned differently. Neither would ever compete in the other's market.

In 1948 the world's first instant camera, the Polaroid Land Camera Model 95, was demonstrated. Management bravely decided to price it at $89.75, against Kodak's Baby Brownie, priced at $2.75. The entire inventory of fifty-six cameras sold on the first day — and Polaroid was launched.

— *SOURCE:* AMA MANAGEMENT REVIEW

How much are you worth? When you work for yourself you have the joy and anguish of deciding what you are worth, then telling your clients.

You can take some lessons from the traditional job market. If you worked for the same employer for many years, you may have received incremental increases — but never huge increases. The reason is that they always remember you as that younger person who walked in the door so many years ago. Remember the power of those early perceptions that affect later inputs.

That's why it is often easier to get a raise by going to a new employer — because you start at a new first impression with them. But even then they want to know what you were paid at your previous employer so they can peg you and only pay a little more.

When you set your pricing, forget what your previous employer paid you. Instead, set your price based on the *total value* you bring to your clients. Remember, *total value = real value + perceived value.*

What if you choose to have the lowest prices in the market? If you are known for low prices, you will never be known for offering the best quality. We expect to pay more for quality. If you were offered a Rolls-Royce for the price of a Chevy, you would probably be very suspicious.

If we are presented with products at a few price levels — $1,000, $3,000, and $5,000 — we will assume the latter product is better. It must be better — it costs more.

Print a price sheet for your main services. Don't try to get every variation on one page. Print it on good quality paper, if not your letterhead.

Pin it on the wall in your office. This will help you remember and get used to how exorbitant your prices may sound. (Whatever your fees, someone will think they are exorbitant, and someone else will think them too cheap.) When you send or fax a price sheet, it looks official. If it looks official, you must be worth it. You must believe in your prices or your prospects will whittle you down, or worse, not buy. What really hurts is when you think you lose a deal on price, and the customer ends up paying more elsewhere.

What to include on your fee schedule

expiry date
payment terms
description of service with accompanying rate
written guarantee

When you are asked your price, answer, "My price is . . ." Then shut up and wait. Let the prospect speak next. Sometimes you might want to justify your price or offer to lower it. Just keep your mouth shut.

If they fall off the chair and say, "Wow!", respond with, "I have been advised to raise it."

If they say that is way out of their range, respond with, "What is your range?"

Then ask who they've had do this work before. Were they very satisfied with that company? If not, why not? Then follow with, "What do I have to do to satisfy you?"

If you are asking $1,000 and they are offering $100, clearly there is no middle ground. If they had $700 in mind, then you can suggest an unbundling of service for $850. You might also offer that you know someone else who might do it for that price, or a junior colleague who is new to the business. Offer it as an alternative — don't be arrogant. Recognize that not everyone can afford your rates. Someday they might.

It hurts to turn down business, but most of the time it pays off in the long run. When you state your price, don't give away ground by calling

Introductory offer ?

the prices "regular," "corporate," "standard," "list," etc., unless you are purposely making it easy for them to negotiate you down.

If you set your price — set it. You might negotiate. Everything is negotiable, but never give something for nothing. If you automatically lower your price, they will come to know you for not being worth your full price. I know of a consultant whose business card states, "Rates Negotiable." What is that person selling? Not quality.

If you are asked to lower your price, and you really want the business, ask the prospect how they can make up the difference in value. Find something of value to trade for. That way if another potential customer asks them your price, they will not embarrass you by quoting a low price, which would make you appear to be ripping the new customer off with your true rates.

If you need to lower your prices, look for justifiable reasons — bulk orders, repeat business, reciprocal business, pilot program, anniversary special, slow period discounts, etc.

Print on your invoice the special reason for the discount — to remind the customer of the great deal you gave them. Also, you don't want them or someone else to look at that invoice much later and assume that is your standard price. It can help make your customer look good to their boss if they can show the regular price and the great deal they negotiated.

THE POWER OF COMPROMISE

A client in the photography business wanted me to speak at their annual sales meeting. They could not afford my rate and suggested that I lower my price. I asked about their program and sounded interested in what they were doing. I was building value by showing my interest in them. I suggested that if there was some way they could make up the difference between their budget and my price we might make a deal. They did by throwing in some camera equipment. They were happy. They stayed within budget and got a first-class speaker they could not normally afford.

— *GEORGE*

No Charge

When you provide a service of value and do not charge for it, make sure you remind the client of the value. If it is warranty service, send them an invoice for the full value of the work, with the words "Covered by warranty." If it was not covered under normal warranty but you decided to eat the cost, write a note across the bottom of the invoice, saying "We cover this one." If you were asked to do a favour, send the client an invoice stating the total value and mark it "No charge." If you think they have a sense of humour write, "Some day I will ask you for a big favour — *Signed, the Godfather.*"

Never let clients think they got something for nothing. Let them know that this time they were very lucky to get something of great value at no cost.

If there is some part of your service you do not charge for, such as a no-charge estimate, evaluation, follow-up meeting, or training session, make sure you tell prospects that, in your written materials and in conversations. And always list the free stuff on the invoice to remind them of everything they received.

> When customers get a good deal from you,
> make sure they know how great it was.

Positioning

You might offer an exclusive product in your lineup. In fact, it might be so exclusive that no one ever orders it. Is that bad? No, if it improves the perception of your line.

THE POWER OF POSITIONING

To market my training business, I had a very classy brochure designed. It describes a two-day seminar for groups of up to twelve senior managers, with two top instructors. The investment is $18,000.

How many have I sold? Not too many. How many will I sell? It doesn't really matter.

> You see, many prospects say, "Wow, that is a lot of money." I reply, "It is. Do you need two instructors?" "Probably not," they answer. "In that case, I can give you a better price with only one." I give them a first-class seminar for much less than $18,000, and they feel good about the deal they got.
> — *Peter*

If you are in the car-cleaning business, you might offer an exclusive Rolls-Royce service package. A client with a BMW or Jag would not object to the Rolls service, would they? Of course you would charge them a little less for their Jag than you would for a Rolls. Wouldn't they feel good! They get Rolls-Royce quality for a Jag price.

> We're overpaying him but he's worth it.
> — *Samuel Goldwyn*

Raising your price

State an expiry date on your price sheet. That tells your clients that you review your prices regularly, say, every six or twelve months. You don't *have* to increase them. You might only adjust parts of your schedule.

Add value to the service when you increase the price. The value might be in improved warranty, faster service, or better quality.

Another way to increase the price is to add a new category of product. The Japanese car industry worked for decades to improve the image and value of their cars. Then to make the next leap they introduced their luxury lines, with a corresponding jump in price. Toyota added Lexus and Honda came out with Acura. It would have been very tough for luxury car buyers to see Toyota and Honda competing with BMW and Mercedes. But Lexus and Acura fit in quite well.

If you are a consultant, your value may increase when you write a book, become known as the expert in your field, win an award, earn a professional designation, serve a new industry, receive media exposure, or complete a bigger project. The law of supply and demand applies. When you get more clients calling you, you are more valuable.

You may feel guilty about raising your fees, even if you think you deserve it. The first time you announce your new rate, you may wince a bit. That's normal. We ask ourselves, "How could I charge so much?" This is common among those who left the corporate world to go into consulting and charge ten times or more a day than what they were paid on salary.

Surgeons are considered well paid. But compared to the value of what they do — saving lives — they are underpaid. They are not paid for their time in the operating room. They are paid for the time, knowledge, and experience they bring with them to every operation.

Similarly, you are not paid for the time you work on the client's project. You are paid for the education, insight, and years of experience you bring to the project. Your clients are paying not for the cost of your time, but for the value of what they receive from your work.

> Whatever is in short supply and high demand
> will increase in value.

RISK

Offer a money-back guarantee. This might be risky for you, but it shows that you are removing some of the risk from your client. Will someone cheat you? Maybe. You can make your guarantee conditional on their looking you in the eye and stating that they were unsatisfied with your service. You can choose your customers. You may decide not to deal with someone you distrust. One of the advantages of being an entrepreneur is that you can choose whom you will do business with.

> As an entrepreneur you have the right to work half-days,
>   six days a week.
> But remember that a full day has twenty-four hours.
> You can work either of the twelve hours that you choose.

1.4 CREDIBILITY

I am only an average man,
but I work harder at it than the average man.
— *THEODORE ROOSEVELT*

To establish and maintain your credibility, you must answer the following questions for your clients and prospects (even though they may not ask the questions out loud).

Your client will ask:

- Are you serious about your business?
- Are you a contender?
- Will I actually like doing business with you?
- Can you really do the work?
- Will you do the work to my satisfaction and on time?
- Are you going to be around next month or next year when I need help?
- Do I even believe you at all?
- Will I regret doing business with you?

Your *actions* will answer those questions.

- Be consistent.
- Be honest.
- Be professional in your approach.
- Be obsessive about some part of your product and service delivery.
- Be the same person to everyone — do not put on airs.
- Be known for the work you do.
- Be known for the satisfied customers who talk and write about you.
- Be known by the company you keep.

We judge you by the people you hang around with. Do you hang with successful entrepreneurs, movers and shakers, business and community leaders, or . . . losers?

▌ Your friends are exactly the way you are or would like to be.

WHEN CREDIBILITY IS OF PRIMARY IMPORTANCE
You need to take action to establish your credibility when

- you start your business
- you move to a new town
- you approach a new prospect
- you enter a new industry
- you add a new product line
- the contact you used to deal with at your customer's company has changed
- you fail to deliver as promised
- you experience bad press or foul rumours.

Every time something changes between you and your market, you need to re-establish credibility. It is harder to establish credibility than to maintain it. But you still need to work to keep your positive image.

MOVING INTO NEW TERRITORY
They said I was crazy when I announced, "I want to teach night school at college."

My friends warned, "Why would anyone hire you? More teachers have just been laid off; they're in a better position than you to get those night school courses. You don't have a degree. And you know nothing about teaching — you're a salesman. Plus, you don't need the hassle or the money of a part-time job on top of your day job."

With encouragement like that it would be easy to be discouraged. Instead I became more determined. I approached this like any other sale.

I sent a letter to the Dean in the business departments at twelve local colleges.

"Congratulations on offering your students programs in sales and marketing. These skills are very important in the business world today. I offer to share my experience with your sales and marketing students through teaching one of your courses. I assure you, I am not a retired salesman looking for something to do. I am a young dynamic salesman eager to share the latest in sales and marketing with your students."

I followed up with a phone call to each Dean inviting them to lunch with me. This resulted in four lunches. After lunch with Dean Sutton of Ryerson I asked, "When do I start?" He laughed and replied, "You sure do practise what you preach."

The first course I taught at Ryerson was a sales course entitled "Effective Persuasion." Over my twelve years as a part-time instructor, I also taught "Marketing for Bankers," "Introduction to Canadian Business," and finally, the big fear for me, "Public Speaking." Teaching the public speaking course is what led me to start my career as a professional speaker many years ago.

— *PETER*

When Coke changed their formula, they did some major scrambling and spending to re-establish credibility for Coke Classic. When McDonald's added pizza, they invested heavily in marketing to establish credibility for the new product and maintain their existing lines.

OTHER WAYS TO IMPROVE YOUR CREDIBILITY
Develop your oral and written communication skills
As an entrepreneur, you are your business. Your prospects judge you in everything you do before they do business with you. How you communicate your message is as important as the message. Often *how you say* something has much more impact than *what you say*. Too many fail because they do not express themselves clearly and confidently.
Volunteer
Get involved with associations or community or charity groups to enhance your visibility and introduce yourself to prospects in a non-selling atmosphere.

ORAL COMMUNICATION

When you're speaking on the phone, in meetings, or one-to-one, listen to how you sound. Are you loud enough to be heard, clear enough to be understood, and succinct enough to make your point? Your enunciation and pronunciation send messages about your background and education. Are they sending the right message? Practise words that you tend to mispronounce.

Your tone often determines how your words are heard. Was your tone angry, tired, anxious, or defensive, or was it positive, friendly, trustworthy, and confident? Television and movies use music to quickly set the tone for a scene. When you speak, all you have is your voice.

Remember that communicating is a two-way process. Listening is a skill, too. In general, people do not tend to listen well; it's something we all must work on. From my meetings with many CEOs of successful corporations, I have discovered that they have at least two things in common — they ask good questions and they listen well. They do not pretend to know everything.

THE 30-SECOND MESSAGE

Distill your main messages into 30-second bites. Often, that's all the time you will have to attract someone's attention. You must make every second count. In his book, *How to Get Your Point Across in 30 Seconds or Less*, Milo Frank describes how to create your 30-second messages. Follow this five-step process:

1. Know your Objective
   What is the result you want from speaking to this person?
2. Know your listener(s)
   What are their needs, concerns, and hot buttons? They do not care what you want. You must help them get what they want.
3. Design your approach
   How will you explain your point? Paint a word picture or use a simple analogy.
4. Hook 'em
   Capture their interest immediately with a question or humour. Both are powerful.

I need to develop this

5. Demand Action

Do not keep them guessing. State clearly what you want them to do next. Buy this product, order today, call me by Friday, join the association, donate $100 to this charity.

Do all that in 30 seconds? Can't be done, you say? Watch TV ads — in 30 seconds that is exactly what they do. But it takes work. You must write, rewrite, and rehearse. Then when the time comes and a prospect gives you 30 seconds, you can give them your best 30 seconds.

Here is a sample 30-second message.

"Our greatest fear is speaking in public. The second greatest fear is dying. Why is it that many would rather be dead in the coffin than delivering the eulogy? If you want to keep your managers from dying on their feet, hire me to do an in-house seminar on presentation skills. Call me now to book your date."

Now create several of your own 30-second messages. Have them rehearsed and ready for action when you need them.

PRESENTATION SKILLS

Get used to speaking in front of others. You might get two minutes at a networking meeting or you may be asked to present a lengthy proposal to a management committee.

HOW TO IMPROVE YOUR PRESENTATION SKILLS
- Study the book *Secrets of Power Presentations*, by Peter Urs Bender
- Enroll in a Dale Carnegie course
- Check out continuing education courses at local colleges
- Join Toastmasters
- Join ITC (International Training in Communications)
- Take a seminar or course on presentation skills
- Practise, practise, practise.

Whenever you speak, ask a trusted colleague to give you honest feedback. Note the words "trusted" and "honest." You want to learn from your strengths and weaknesses. You do not want to be destroyed or flattered. Ask what you can improve. If they say you were good, ask what they enjoyed the most. If they still say you were good, ask them to recommend you to another audience.

WRITTEN COMMUNICATION

You are what you write. Your writing represents you in letters, memos, notes, articles, and e-mail.

Do

Be clear and concise.
Be specific.
Use spell-check software.
Use simple language that everyone can understand.
Use questions to make the writing interesting and engaging.
Take a writing course.
Read books on writing.
Have someone edit your material for grammar and style.

Avoid

Jargon (technical, industry, trade)
Long sentences
Long paragraphs

You are judged by how you present your ideas. Clear, sharp writing conveys professional attention to detail and time. Vagueness creates distrust and wastes everyone's time.

If you look at every message you write as having the potential to make or lose a sale, you will put more thought and skill into writing.

VOLUNTEER WORK

Many large companies donate their senior executives' time to major charities such as the United Way. The executives get their names and pictures in the media, and that's free, positive publicity. The more humane a company looks, the more ready people — and other companies, run by people — are to do business with them.

Big companies take pains to show that they care. You have a big advantage as a small business owner, because it is a lot easier to believe that you care. In the business world we tend to believe the small guys care. We tend to think that the big guys are too big to care.

You might not have the time to get involved with a charity's major fundraising campaign. But you might choose to participate in some other way. Pick a cause that you believe in, not one that you think will get you the most publicity.

The Body Shop supports various environmental and social causes. They use their retail stores to display information posters about their chosen causes. They receive payback in multiple ways. They have won many community, business, social, and environmental awards. They get free media coverage — so much that they do not need to advertise. Their customers feel good about shopping in their stores. Their customers are loyal. Their employees feel good about working there. And they create change that goes beyond just profit and jobs.

THE POWER OF VOLUNTEERISM

I met with the president of The Body Shop Canada, Margot Franssen. My first question was, "What business are you in?" Without pause she answered, "We are in the communication business. We communicate through our actions, products, and words in order to effect social change. It's what we do well. We use our shops to communicate with the public." I reminded her that they sell body-care products. Franssen replied, "It's not what you sell. It's how you manufacture it and what you do with the money you make."

The Body Shop is very effective in advancing the causes they support. They are also profitable.

— *GEORGE*

BUSINESS ASSOCIATIONS

Be seen in the public eye. Appear as a spokesperson for your association or local Chamber of Commerce. Becoming the president of your trade association adds to your credibility. You will have even more positive exposure if you are the public relations person.

1.5 EXPERTISE *Be the Expert*

| It is lonely at the top — but the lunches are better.

Credibility is important, but it is even better to be seen as "the expert." When you are believed to be the expert,

- customers come to you
- it is easier to get through the corporate gatekeepers
- people like to hang around with you
- it is easier to make breakfast and lunch appointments
- you can charge higher fees
- you attract a more exclusive class of business
- you have more opportunities to pick and choose your business
- you spend more time doing what you are really good at and enjoy
- the media may be interested in your opinion
- you receive more referrals from your peers
- others will use you as a benchmark against which to measure themselves.

There are also disadvantages to being "the expert." For example,

- others may be jealous
- some love to see experts have their faces rubbed in the mud
- people expect more from you
- lesser mortals will ask you for free help
- strangers may approach you when you don't want to be approached.

But all things considered, becoming an expert is a goal worth pursuing. Here are some tips on how to make your way there.

FOCUS OR SPECIALIZE

Who is perceived as a better doctor: a GP or a neurosurgeon? Who makes more money? Who gets more referrals from their colleagues? Both are honourable professions, and both can be happy. But where do you want to be in your field? The toughest part about specializing is that you will have to give up some things in order to focus. It may take some sacrifice, but you will have to narrow your field of expertise and get very good at it.

> We can do whatever we want in life.
> But we cannot do everything we want in life.
> — *GEORGE TOROK'S GRANDFATHER*

> Where your talents and the world's needs cross,
> there lies your vocation.
> — *ARISTOTLE*

SETTING DIRECTION

You may already know where you plan to focus. Sometimes the market opens doors of opportunity, and you have to be ready to go through those doors. Seizing the opportunity might even require that you adjust your specialty.

SPECIALIZING — BY ACCIDENT

Soon after I came to Canada, I was enjoying a beer one night in a bar in Banff, Alberta. An old native man in the group I was with offered me some strange advice. "If you ever have to jump on a running horse," he said, "jump on it in the direction it is going." "What a ridiculous idea," I thought. "Why would I ever jump on a running horse?"

Years later that idea came back to help me. I was visiting my parents' home in Switzerland and received a call from a friend in

Canada. He said, "Bender, you made it! You are on the front page of the business section of *The Toronto Star*. They called you the "Presentations Guru."

Just before my holiday, I had finally landed an interview with a business writer for *The Toronto Star*. I was in the midst of writing a book on marketing. However, the interviewer wanted to talk about giving presentations (which I also did), so that's what we talked about.

When I heard about the article, I remembered the old man's story. The running horse, in this case, was my new status as the "Presentations Guru." So I jumped. I decided to change my focus, and wrote a book on the secrets of giving power presentations instead.

— PETER

WRITE   write in colums ⇒ experts

One of the best ways to become known as the expert is to write. You could write to — or for — newsletters (association, corporate, community), newspapers (community, business, trade, weekly, daily), or magazines (general, trade, association, business).

WRITE A LETTER TO THE EDITOR

This is the easiest way to be published. Watch for an issue that you feel strongly about or that touches your business. The issue doesn't have to relate to your business. This is just a chance for people to know you. Take a stand. If you can make your communication funny, that is even better. Write it well. The editors will correct grammar and edit for length. Sign the letter with your name and a moniker that you like, or your business name. If you find nothing gets your juices flowing enough to write a letter of opinion, write to the editor to say what you like about the publication. They always print those letters.

WRITE A LETTER TO A COLUMNIST OR WRITER

Sometimes columnists never get mail, and they will love you if you actually write them a letter. Pick a columnist or columnists that you like. If you like them, there is a pretty good chance that they are similar to you in some way, and they will like you.

WRITE AN ARTICLE

Even if you think you can't write, write. Then edit your work by rewriting it again and again, until it sounds good. No one ever will know how many times you rewrote. When you admire a movie you never judge it by how many takes it took to get the shot, or by the film left on the editing room floor. When others read your article they only see the finished product, not the rewrites.

Ideas for Articles

How you learned the importance of . . .
How you got started in the business . . .
Your worst customer service experience . . .
Your favourite customer . . .
The best lesson you learned last year . . .
Something funny that happened to you . . .

Or, how about writing a list? I've found these to be very valuable.

Tips	*Warnings*
the number one principle for success . . .	the single biggest fallacy . . .
two ways of approaching . . .	two dangers of . . .
three questions to ask when buying . . .	three wrong turns made by . . .
four cornerstones of . . .	four common mistakes . . .
five key elements of . . .	the five myths . . .
six steps to creating a . . .	six major obstacles . . .
seven ways to save money . . .	seven deadly sins . . .
ten tips when using . . .	ten ways to waste . . .

With your article, include your name, phone number, e-mail address, and short bio describing your specialty. Try to get your photo published. Send it with your article and ask them to include it. Make this easy — get black-and-white 5 x 7s, and print at least fifty copies, so you'll have them on hand for future uses.

WRITE A COLUMN

If you write a column, you must be an expert. Writing a column is a lot like writing articles, only more frequently. Your column might run weekly, monthly, or quarterly. You must contribute regularly and there must be a theme to the column that runs through each article. Work a regular "writing time" into your schedule. Then sit down and write no matter how little you feel like doing it at that time. You will train your mind and body that this is your writing time. If you commit to writing a column, never let your editor down. To be safe, always be a couple of columns ahead. If you think you might not meet the schedule, find a co-columnist or line up some guest columnists to be on standby. They get exposure and it boosts your image by associating you with other "experts." Remember that if you hang around with experts, you must be one yourself.

It won't take long for you to to have enough columns to fill a booklet — a nice value-added item you can provide to your clients. Write enough columns and you have a whole book. If you have been writing a column for a long time, you can start printing a "best of" compilation.

Encourage your readers to write to you with their questions, opinions, or requests. Offer them a gift if they write — one of your booklets, or a free consultation.

Do all the self-promotion with your column that you would for your articles (see above). With a column you have more bargaining power — insist on your photo being used.

One of the best ways to be perceived as an expert is for the media to treat you like an expert. Arrange to be interviewed by the media, and get on their "expert" list; in other words, be the person they call when they need an opinion on your topic. See Chapter 3 for countless tips on working with the media, and concrete advice on becoming their "expert on call."

CONDUCT A SURVEY

National polling companies make a lot of money conducting political, product, and social issue surveys. Polling is an inexact science, and purchasing the survey research from these companies can be very expensive. If you need specific information related to your business or your customers, you can conduct your own simple survey without spending too much money. And, more to the point, you can use the results of your surveys to get your name in the news.

A survey can give you research data that you can interpret and publish. Send it to the press; they may print it and interview you. As an extra bonus, the people who participated in the survey become prospects. And you gain the credibility of being associated with the survey. If it works once, repeat it — quarterly or yearly. Note the success of the quarterly U.S. Purchasing Managers Index, published by the National Association of Purchasing Managers. The index gets quoted in all the top U.S. business papers. Another successful annual survey is Blackwell's list of the best- and worst-dressed celebrities. It is just his opinion. He doesn't even bother doing the work of a survey. Yet he gets tons of free exposure. Can you create a list of the best or worst in your industry?

Design a simple two- or three-question survey that relates to your business. Find a paper or association that will partner with you and publish your results. Use the partner's name to enhance the credibility of your research. If you indicate that you're "conducting a survey for the President's Association" (or whatever association is involved), you are more likely to get a response.

The simpler your survey, the better. The easiest survey is to ask a few people some questions and and state your results. The problem with this approach, however, is that it has no credibility.

Here are some simple steps to follow when conducting a survey:

1. The most important step is planning. Decide what you want to do with the results, especially if you find you don't like the conclusion. If you have more than one purpose, clearly understand your primary goal and prioritize any others. This makes the survey easier to design.

2. Describe the group you plan to poll and how many replies you need to show credible results.

3. Decide how you will collect the survey — on the street, on the phone, over coffee, by fax, by mail, over the Internet, etc.

4. Design your questionnaire, then try completing it yourself. Test it on a few others. Is it clear and simple to complete? The fewer questions you ask, the more likely it is that people will reply. The higher up the executive hierarchy your respondents are, the shorter your questionnaire had better be.

5. Design your process for compiling and analyzing. For your results to be credible, your target audience must understand and trust your results.

6. Plan the best time to conduct it, and the best time to start and finish.

7. Conduct the survey. Do it yourself or hire someone.

8. Compile and analyze your results. Form conclusions.

9. Publish the results.

10. Review the process. What would you do differently next time? Would you do it again?

If the survey will take a lot of time, hire some students to collect and compile results. Or arrange with the local business school for their students to do the survey as a project.

One very effective way to conduct a survey (and gain prospects) is by calling CEOs on the phone and asking for five minutes of their time. Tell them you are conducting a poll of leaders in their industry. For their participation you will keep their names confidential and will share the overall results with them (leaders want to know what other leaders are thinking). Ask them no more than two or three questions.

Henry Luce's creation of *Fortune* magazine in 1929 spawned the Fortune 500, which became the corporate benchmark for the twentieth century. It was a clever marketing technique for the magazine.

SPONSOR
Sponsoring is a friendly way of advertising.

Sponsorship Opportunities

an award

a contest

a special event

a sports team (pro, amateur, or youth)

a library room or book collection

park equipment or a flower bed

a charity

a radio or TV show

a cultural exchange

a business dinner

a community fundraiser

a youth program

a parade float

SPONSOR A DOOR PRIZE

Who could use a door prize? Any group that holds a gathering, whether it is a breakfast, lunch, dinner, banquet, seminar, conference, or golf tournament. If your prospects might be there, donate a door prize. If they meet every month, donate enough for every month for the whole year. Try to get listed in the program as a sponsor. You have more clout to negotiate for recognition if your contribution is regular or large.

You don't need to attend every meeting yourself, but if you are a sponsor, the participants will hear your name at every meeting — and some lucky person will be delighted with your prize. If you do attend, ask to present the prize yourself. Don't be the one to draw the winning name, because those who do not win will blame you for picking the *wrong* name.

You don't have to belong to the group to donate a door prize — just ask. Always attach your card or label with your name and number to the prize. The prize could be related to what you sell, but it doesn't have to be. Set up a small display near the entrance announcing the door prize and showing you as sponsor.

Offer your product as a sponsor prize

SPONSOR AN AWARD

Contact the local high schools, colleges, and universities to find out whether they have a contest that might be appropriate for you to sponsor. Speak to the dean, principal, or department head. If they're too busy, you may do better by talking directly with the department heads or teachers. If nothing suitable exists, suggest that you would sponsor an award if they would organize it.

SPONSOR A CONTEST   *CONTEST*

Create your own contest. This is similar to the award but it is more like an event-plus-award opportunity. This is a great way to get annual recognition and feel good about what you do. Students are a natural target audience for contests. They need money, and small amounts of money go further for students than they do for adults.

MORE THOUGHTS ON SPONSORING

When you have a choice between advertising or sponsoring, choose to sponsor. Advertising looks like advertising: it's obviously self-serving. Sponsoring shows that you care. It can cost less than advertising and give you more.

You can sponsor by:

1. conduct a survey
2. sponsor a contest
3. offer to speak at diff. functions

- paying money
- contributing your time
- offering a prize
- donating a product
- offering display space
- bartering
- endorsing.

SPONSOR ANNUAL EVENTS

If you sponsor or run an event, survey, or award, and it does well, do it every year. It could become part of the local culture. The town of Fergus, Ontario, closed off the main street and invited families to bring their favourite teddy bears downtown. It went so well they made it an annual event. Every year these events are easier to organize. You learn from your mistakes, and others will offer to help.

JUDGE A CONTEST

Call the local schools and colleges to find out what contests they need judges for.

Offer to judge a student competition. Donate something for the winners. Happy students tell their parents about what they won.

EARN CERTIFICATIONS AND DEGREES

Some are impressed when you earn a Ph.D., MBA, or other degree. It adds to your credibility. If you've got it, use it. But remember it only helps; it does not make the sale.

Almost every field has a professional certification. Achieving it tells your customers that your peers recognize you as an expert. You may be seen as better for having completed the program.

WIN AWARDS AND SPECIAL RECOGNITION

Many municipalities and associations honour their person of the year. You might not make the *Time* magazine "Man of the Year," but you can put your name forward for local and regional awards. Often they ask for submissions. Just call your city hall for information. Fill out the form and send it in. If you win the award, proudly display it and let your customers and prospects know.

Even if you do not win, make like the movie business and announce that you were nominated. Movies are publicized as having been "nominated for seven Academy Awards"; they never tell you they didn't win any.

Contact the small business help centres for more information. Check with business publications and the business editors of your community newspapers to find out more about local awards.

SPEAK IN PUBLIC

Offer to speak to organizations for free. Polish your speaking skills so you will be recommended and called back. Almost every organization needs speakers, although not all of them will be right for you and not all of them will want you.

Try to target organizations where you might have prospects. Consider the speech a chance to deliver an infomercial in front of prime prospects. Now, it can't be a straight commercial. You must provide information of value to the audience. You're probably thinking, "Give it away for free? Am I nuts?" Give them tidbits of value — not everything. If you are good they will be interested in hiring you.

You might not get the audiences you want interested in you. In that case just start speaking somewhere. It is good practice. Eventually word gets around that you are available for speaking and that you are a good speaker. You help spread it of course.

Do get good at speaking. See the notes earlier in this chapter under "Credibility."

WHERE TO SPEAK?

Any group that holds weekly, monthly, or quarterly meetings needs speakers. Other opportunities for speakers are banquets, trade shows, seminars, and conferences.

Here are some groups that often need speakers:

Business Groups
Networking clubs
Trade and professional associations
Chamber of Commerce
Board of Trade
Jaycees (Junior Chamber of Commerce)
Junior Achievement

Service Clubs
Rotary
Lions/Lionesses Club
Optimist Club
Kinsmen/Kinettes
Kiwanis

Community Groups
Public library
Schools, colleges, universities
Community centres
Churches, synagogues, and temples
Canadian Club
Empire Club

These are just a few ideas. Find more by checking with city hall or the library for a list of associations in your town. Watch for notices of group meetings. Call the groups to offer yourself as a speaker. You may wish to attend some of these functions to see how they are run, and the level of speaker and audience they have and expect.

Every trade or profession has its own association — often more than one. Consider the groups that represent accountants, lawyers, project managers, secretaries, buyers, dentists, salespeople, technicians, etc.

Check the library for the association directories. You will be amazed at how many associations there are. Every association has an annual conference and monthly or quarterly events at which they may need speakers. If you speak for the local chapter, you might also try other chapters and the regional and national groups.

Some associations maintain a list of members who are willing to speak. Check the ones you belong to — or might join — and get on their speaker lists. *Do you have a speakers list*

Speak to the associations that your clients belong to. Ask your clients if you can use their name as a reference.

WHAT TO SAY?

One of the easiest ways to give a speech is to list and answer the most common questions asked about your business. This is good because you know it so well. See the above discussion of written skills, under "Credibility," for more ideas. What applies to writing an article or letter applies to a speech.

Don't forget to give the audience what they want or are interested in. It's important that your speech not be a sales pitch.

MAKING THE MOST OF YOUR PUBLIC SPEAKING

Send notices of your speech to your clients, prospects, and the media. When speaking at a conference or program with a printed flyer or brochure, make sure your name and photo are included. This gives your presentation additional value. If you are not charging a fee for your speech, insist that your program is listed with a note — "sponsored by." You find a company to name as your sponsor. It might be a good client or a colleague. It doesn't cost them or you anything to add the note, but to those reading the program you look like a valuable speaker because someone sponsored you.

After your speech, ask for a testimonial letter from the organizers. Use these letters to get more speeches.

I heard of one professional speaker who, whenever he does a training program for a company, asks them for a little bit more. He will do a presentation to a local school — sponsored by the client. The client gets community goodwill. The school and students get a professional speaker they could never afford. The speaker gets a bit more money and he does something good.

Make your free speeches look more valuable. After your speech send the organization an invoice for your time. Yes, an invoice. But since the speech was free, handwrite in big letters on the invoice, "Fee waived!" They will know that they didn't get a free speech — they got a donation of your service and expertise.

But you are not a professional speaker. How much should you charge for a speech? You could bill at your regular hourly consulting rate. But I suggest that if your hourly consulting rate is $100, an hour-long speech should be worth $500. Why? It is more stressful to make a speech. When you consult, you normally work one-on-one. When speaking, you are really consulting one-to-many, so the organizers get more value.

BE KNOWN IN THE PRESS

We believe what we hear and read in the press. The more you can get the press to talk about you, the more credible and important you appear to be. If the press calls you the expert, it must be true — even if you have to help them give you that label! See Chapter 3, "Media," for more on developing relationships with the press.

THE MEDIA CALLED ME A "CITIZEN OF THE WORLD"

I didn't plan it, but I helped it happen. A local newspaper columnist asked residents to write about why they liked our community, Burlington. I responded that I liked the international links our community had. For my family, especially my three children, these included the annual youth sports exchange with Burlington, Vermont; a football exchange with Cincinnati, Ohio; and an exchange with Itabashi, Japan. I listed several other international links, including my own travels around the world and virtual travel via computer networks.

I signed the letter "George Torok, a Citizen of the World." The columnist liked my letter so much that she sent a photographer to take a picture of my whole family, and ran the photo with my letter. The article was headed with the title "Citizen of the World."

Now I can tell others that the media called me a "Citizen of the World." I just don't tell them that the idea came from me.

— *GEORGE*

| Beauty is in the eye of the beholder.

Your product and service may be beautiful, but if people do not know about it or do not see it, it is up to you to "glam" it up and step into the spotlight. Life isn't fair. You must be good and be seen to be good.

Muhammad Ali was a great boxer. There have been other great boxers. But no one was as great a self-promoter as Ali. He built his career and the boxing industry through shameless promotion.

| Float like a butterfly. Sting like a bee.
| — *MUHAMMAD ALI*

It can be tough to sell and market yourself. After all, it seems like bragging, and your parents may have taught you to be "modest." They might have bragged about you behind your back — that was okay. But bragging about yourself was frowned upon.

I remember growing up with another set of rules: go to school, study hard, get good marks, get a good job working for a good company, and the company will look after you. I wanted to believe in those rules, but I found that reality isn't so conscientious. I had to rethink whether what my parents and teachers had taught me still applied.

The reality is that you must promote yourself. Get over the fear, and get on with it.

> Our deepest fear is not that we are inadequate.
> Our deepest fear is that we are powerful beyond measure.
> It is our light, not our darkness, that most frightens us.
> We ask ourselves, who am I to be brilliant, gorgeous,
> talented and fabulous?
> Actually, who are you not to be?
> — *NELSON MANDELA IN HIS 1994 INAUGURAL ADDRESS*

SUMMARY
SECRETS OF PERCEPTIONS

- Look for and manage your unintended messages. They have as much (maybe more) impact as your conscious messages.
- Create positive first impressions *every* time — with your smile, hand-shake, business card, and appearance.
- Listen to your voice mail message with a critical ear and impatient mindset. Then improve it to project a positive experience for your caller. Review periodically.
- Deliver value and make them aware of all that you give. Emphasize the perceived value for more effective marketing.
  Total value = Real value + Perceived value.
- Enhance your credibility as an expert through public speaking and writing. Improve that expert image with contests, surveys, awards, and special recognition.

Add this to 12 wks Manual.

Strong relationships with your clients and prospects
will earn you more business than price and quality alone.
— George Torok

Relationships

The only things worth counting on
are people you can count on.
— *Dwight D. Eisenhower*

Okay. In case you haven't heard, marketing is about people, people, people. People make decisions — buying decisions — and anyone marketing a product should realize that. In recent years, business has changed from mass production and mass merchandising to customization to personalization, as leaders become aware that everyone wants to be treated as unique.

The faster technology moves, the more it automates our lives, and the less human contact is required. Technology gives us more choices. Too many choose to become impersonal. But the need for human contact does not diminish just because technology is changing. Therein lies the opportunity for you. Neither technology nor corporations have relationships — people do.

How can you nurture positive relationships?

- Be honest.
- Be friendly.
- Make others feel special.
- Be consistent.
- Build trust.
- Be helpful.

- Appear interested.
- Show respect.
- Be yourself.
- Be unique.
- Stay in touch.
- Be easy to reach.
- Respond to queries quickly.
- Display a sense of humour.
- Be considerate.
- Don't waste time.

Can you do all that?

Keeping relationships alive and well is not easy. But it builds a stronger sustainable business.

> I am Anonymous. Help me!
> — *GRAFFITI*

> It takes twenty years to build a reputation and five minutes to ruin it.
> If you think about that you'll do things differently.
> — *WARREN BUFFETT*

Fundamentally, in order to have a good relationship with someone, you have to like them, and they have to like you. It's been shown, and it makes sense, that we tend to like people who are similar to us in some way, whether because of a shared nationality, background, hobby, political viewpoint, community, religion, professional affiliation, or favourite sport.

So the first step in finding relationships is to find people like you — or to be more like others. Here are just a few places where you might find people like you:

- place of worship
- community centre
- sports teams

- alumni association
- service clubs
- trade association

We like to do business with others from our "club," whether that club is a structured organization or an informal association of likeminded people. Don't be shy to take advantage of your club connections. If it works, use it. If you are not in the club, you just have to find another way of connecting.

I heard the mayor of a large city speaking at a big conference. He started his speech by talking about how long he had known "Sarah," the conference chair. By mentioning this he connected with everyone because we all knew Sarah. Now he had something in common with all of us — and we were ready to listen to what else he had to say.

> Birds of a feather flock together.
> Find ways to highlight the common feathers.

It doesn't take a lot to establish a bond with others. When I drove my brother's van, other van drivers waved at me. When I rode a motorcycle, other motorcycle riders waved. (Well, not all of them waved; I rode a mid-size Japanese bike, so Harley riders never even acknowledged me.) When I go running, other runners say "Hi."

There are exceptions, of course: When you drive a Rolls-Royce and you wave to other Rolls drivers, none will wave back.

— *GEORGE*

If you appear to be like others, they will like you and listen to you more. How can you be more like other people? Listen and become interested in them. They will like that, and take a reciprocal interest in you.

In this chapter you will find methods to enhance your personal communication skills, make the most of networking opportunities, and manage your group relationships and special relationships.

You may wish to bookmark the action list on pages 110–11. It is too easy to read the list on that page and forget it quickly. The rest of this chapter is chock full of tips, ideas, and examples, but that list should be your touchstone — a List of Golden Rules — for nurturing relationships. You can't review it too often. Whenever you are trying to look for new ways to grow your relationships, return to the list and ask yourself, "How can I be more . . . ?"

One more guiding principle for relationships: feelings. Yes, feelings. Although it is logical to do all the little things that build relationships, it is feelings that keep them alive. A client's relationship with you is based on how they *feel* about you. So don't be surprised to learn that they buy on emotion and justify with logic.

We all make decisions based on how we feel. If you can affect how we feel, you can affect our decisions. Building relationships will have an impact on how we feel about you, your product, and ourselves.

> Always go to other people's funerals;
> otherwise, they won't come to yours.
> — *Yogi Berra*

2.1 PERSONAL COMMUNICATION

> The two secrets of life are flowers and thank yous.
> — *Tom Peters*

Advertising to the masses does not build relationships. Don't get me wrong — advertising does work. But it is expensive and impersonal. To build strong relationships you must get personal. A mass-produced, glitsy flyer may look good but it does not show personal involvement from you. It could have been written, designed, and printed by people you hired.

It's like receiving a birthday card from a new friend. The card was nice but it was addressed to Mary — and your name is Maria.

A small handwritten note to your clients is very personal. It shows you took the time to personally get involved. It's the small things that make an impact. Even a mass mailing can be personalized by attaching a personal note in your handwriting.

THANK YOUS

Send handwritten thank-you notes to your customers, prospects, colleagues, or anyone who does something for you. Don't do it because you have to. Do it because you don't have to. It will make a bigger impression when you do something you don't have to do.

THE POWER OF THANKS

I sponsor an annual speech contest for Grade 12 students. After my third annual contest I received a thank-you letter from one of the student contestants. I was delighted with this letter. Three students took home prize money totalling $5,000. What really impressed me was that I received only one letter — from a student who had not won any money. I remembered that he arrived early the day of the contest, spoke well, and just missed out on the money. He probably should have felt very bad at not winning; instead, he sent me a thank you.

— *PETER*

Saqib Awan
(address confidential)

Peter Urs Bender
108–150 Palmdale Dr.
Toronto, ON M1T 3M7

Dear Mr. Bender:
I would like to take this opportunity to thank you for giving me the chance to participate in the third annual Grade 12 **Peter Urs Bender Public Speaking Contest** on the topic of "Proud To Be Canadian."

It was a notable experience for me as I learned a lot about public speaking and about the best country in the world — Canada. Although I did not win any cash prizes in the contest, I definitely had a great time and cherish every moment of it. I can honestly say that I came out of that room as a winner and will take this experience with me wherever I go. I am also glad to inform you that I am a better presenter today than I was before reading *Secrets of Power Presentations.*

Again, thank you and congratulations on such a splendid job in raising awareness of public speaking and of Canada among youth. Way to go! Please do not hesitate to call me if you have any questions/ comments or need my help with anything in the future. My phone number is (416) 555-****. I would be more than glad to help!

Sincerely,

Saqib Awan

HANDWRITING

Many people are embarrassed or ashamed of their handwriting and are loath to write thank-you cards because of it. As a certified graphologist and graphoanalyst, I assure you that your writing probably has wonderful personality characteristics within it. It is likely that the "messier" your writing appears to be, the more well adjusted you are. Picture-perfect writing — the kind you were taught in school — shows your conventionality. Why not be unique? Those with neat, perfect writing usually have more hang-ups than do those with more original script.

Here are a few tips to incorporate into your writing and signature. By changing your writing you can bring change to your life! If the lines of your writing gently ascend on the page, you are broadcasting your optimism. Joining your t-bars to the next letter and forming figure-eights with g's, f's, and s's indicates your fluidity of mind and your ability to think on your feet. If you use stand-alone t-bars, making them firm demonstrates strong willpower, while making them long shouts enthusiasm. If you underscore your name with one firm line moving from left to right, you are showing self-reliance. Straight downstrokes on your y's indicate your determination.

A handwritten thank-you or personal note will garner more attention than any page of typed characters.

— ELAINE CHARAL, TORONTO, ON, HANDWRITING SPECIALIST

WHY DON'T PEOPLE SEND MORE THANK YOUS?

Is it that they can't be bothered? Do they believe it won't be appreciated, especially if the recipient is someone big and important? Do they think it is a waste of time?

The reality is that everyone likes to be thanked. We hear the words "thank you" so seldom that we remember and feel good about those who do say it. Do you want others to feel good about you?

BEWARE THE NAKED MAN

Harvey Mackay is the president of Mackay Envelope company, the bestselling author of five books, a keynote speaker, and an active community volunteer. He sent copies of his fourth book, *Dig Your Well Before You're Thirsty*, to all 4,000 members of the National Speakers Association.

After reading my copy, I wrote him a note of thanks. In my note I commented on each of his books that I had read. I had not read his second book, so I didn't mention it. I sent my note and figured I would probably never hear from him again.

A few months later I received my letter back, covered with his handwritten notes. He had taken the time from his busy schedule to read my letter and comment on each point. And in addition to my letter he sent me a copy of his second book, *Beware the Naked Man Who Offers You His Shirt* — personally signed.

What amazed me was that he had read my letter, thought about it, and responded. He had also noticed that I did not talk about his second book and rightly assumed that I hadn't read it; hence the free copy. He didn't have to do that, but he did. That's what makes it so special. Every time I tell this story, does it sell a few more books for Harvey?

— *GEORGE*

Say thank you to clients, prospects, colleagues, media, and people of influence for:

- paying the invoice
- the recent project they worked on with you
- past business
- considering your proposal (even if you didn't get it this time)
- meeting with you
- touring you through their facility
- helping you organize the program you delivered
- introducing you to the chairman and vice presidents
- supporting your ideas
- being such a warm host
- the new idea they gave you
- the discussion over lunch
- the lead for that new client
- the constructive feedback on the last job
- *Add some of your own ideas . . .*

There are many ways to say thank you. You could send:

- a post card
- a generic thank-you card
- custom printed cards
- a gift
- e-mail
- a book
- a referral
- a business lead.

You could also send:

- food
- chocolate (chocolate is not food — it is the gift of the gods)
- an article that might be of interest
- information about a seminar, conference, or event they might enjoy
- a free product sample
- a cartoon they might enjoy.

Roz Usherof, an image specialist, once thanked me by buying me a new tie. It was expensive, and she presented it to me in a fancy box. I remember her every time I wear the tie.

SHOWING APPRECIATION

Jim Harris, an author and speaker, has a unique way of saying thank you. Recently, I organized a special post card as a joint promotion for him and three other authors on the topic of leadership.

Soon after, Jim called me for help. "I need to take someone special out for a fancy dinner. Can you recommend your favourite spot?"

Jim called that restaurant to arrange a lovely dinner for me and one guest — to be paid by him. He insisted that the meal include one of their best bottles of wine or champagne (or both) plus a minimum of one rich dessert. Jim gave the restaurant manager his credit card number and authorization to charge everything plus a 20 percent gratuity. He instructed them to mail him the charge slip after the meal.

Jim also mailed me a Certificate of Appreciation. It was printed on certificate paper and mailed in a large envelope so it arrived uncrinkled.

I will enjoy the meal with my wife much more than if Jim had taken us to dinner. And will I feel special and remember him? You bet!

— PETER

CONGRATULATIONS

"Congratulations!" is the first cousin of "Thank you!"

The following example shows the positive results of sending a note of congratulations. Notice the roller coaster of emotions you might experience when you approach someone who is greatly admired for their power, wealth, or position.

THE POWER OF CONGRATULATIONS

I read in a newspaper that a man named Seymour Schulich had given $15 million to York University, and that the university had named its business school after him (the Schulich School of Business). I respect that kind of generosity. So I thought, "Gee, if he can give away so much money, why don't I give him a book?" I took a copy of *Secrets of Power Presentations*, and wrote in it, "Mr. Schulich: Congratulations. We should have more Canadians like you," and sent it to him.

A few weeks later I was in my office and the phone rang. I answered and heard, "Schulich speaking." I got all excited. "I got your book." I was feeling really up! "I read your book." Wow! I was on the ceiling. I felt wonderful.

Then he said, "I don't like your book." My emotions fell. It was like I was on a roller coaster. I felt crushed. I was ready to hang up. I thought, "Who the heck are you to call me on a sunny day and tell me you don't like my book?"

Then Mr. Schulich said, "I love your book." And I was up again! He invited me out to lunch.

A week later, we met, and I was impressed. Not with the lunch, but with the fact that he had read my book and underlined and circled passages throughout. He said, "It's the best work I've ever seen on presentations. As a matter of fact, I think you should go to York University and talk to the teachers and students there."

Since then I have spoken several times at the Schulich School of Business. And the seventh edition of my book contains a copy of a letter from Schulich endorsing the book. I could not have paid him for that kind of endorsement.

It all started with a note of congratulations.

— *PETER*

When someone does something good, applaud!
You will make two people happy.
— *SAMUEL GOLDWYN*

Send notes of congratulations to clients, prospects, movers and shakers, media, and colleagues when they:

- receive an award
- get nominated for an award

Send Thank You + congradulatio notes to clients

- should have been nominated for an award
- reach a milestone (anniversary, goal, project completion, etc.)
- appear in the media
- speak at an event
- announce a new product, office, or employee
- sponsor a charity
- get a promotion
- write an article or book
- launch a new product
- open a new location
- enter a new market
- close a big deal
- invent something
- create something
- enter into a new partnership
- start a new job
- accept a community role
- start a volunteer position
- organize an event
- tried something new — even if it didn't work
- celebrate a family event (birthday, new child, marriage)
- _Add some of your own ideas . . ._

I can live for two months on a good compliment.
— _MARK TWAIN_

NOTES

"Welcome back, hope your tour of Europe was a success"
"Hope your conference was great again this year"
"Good luck on the promotion/proposal/election/new project"

As you can see, there are countless occasions that deserve acknowledgement in the form of a personal note. Build your relationships by noticing these opportunities and acting on them.

CUSTOMIZED NOTE CARDS

NOTE CARDS

Print custom note cards with your name and logo. A simple but effective alternative is to use blank invitation cards. Glue your business card on the front and write your message on the inside. Another variation is to buy cards that you can print from your computer. These come in various paper styles. You can produce something that looks sharp and customized.

AWARDS

Nominate others for awards — in the community, in their association, in their company. Take note of announcements of awards. Ask yourself, "Of the people I know, who may be worthy of that award?" Then inquire about how to nominate that person the next time the award is going to be presented. Tell the nominee what you are doing so you can get more information from them. If you don't tell them, they may never know they were nominated. If you see someone doing something exceptional, suggest that their association or company create an award.

Nominees will appreciate being nominated, and award winners always remember their nominator. If your nominee wins, suggest that they send out a news release. (To make it easier — why not give them a copy of this book?)

If no award exists to honour someone deserving, create your own award on a note card and send it to them.

APOLOGIES

If you are like me, you are not perfect. Sometimes we make mistakes. When we do, we try to learn and we should apologize. Everybody slips up now and then — but not everybody apologizes.

THE POWER OF APOLOGY

You've heard plenty of big bad bank stories; in all likelihood, you've experienced a few of your own. Here's one with a twist.

My bank bounced one of my cheques. My supplier called to inform me. I was greatly annoyed, as I knew my account held ten times the value of the cheque. But as I learned later, this account was less than six months old so they held every deposit for thirty days. The stupid part is that I had had accounts with this bank for twenty years.

Now let me tell you the good part. Realizing their error, the bank apologized to me and sent me a letter. They also apologized to my supplier and sent her a letter stating that they had erred and what a solid, long-standing customer I was.

They did not need to do all that, but they did. And both my supplier and I will remember. We won't forget the stupid error, but we will remember how they fixed it and more.

— *GEORGE*

When you make an error, how far will you go to impress your customer? Do you try to justify why you did what you did and mumble that it wasn't really your fault? Do you simply fix it? Or do you go beyond expectations?

Fix the results, fix the system, satisfy the customer, and tell them what you did. And apologize.

Customers who have problems fixed to their satisfaction tend to be more loyal than those who never experienced a problem. It is almost worthwhile to screw up, just so you can fix it and apologize. They will remember how you went beyond the call of duty and they will tell others. The best form of marketing is to have satisfied customers tell others about you. *Go beyond the Call of Duty when you Mess up!*

DO YOU HAVE A MONEY-BACK GUARANTEE?

If you want to build trust, offer a 100 percent money-back guarantee. And let your customers know about it.

> People talk about two types of service: exceptional and bad.
> The ho-hum doesn't make an impression.

POST CARDS

Post cards are more personal than letters. They are friendlier than flyers, and more likely to get read. Most people read them before other mail, and may even stick them up on the wall.

TOURIST POST CARDS

Buy local post cards with scenes of tourist attractions or landscapes. Send them to clients far away, with a note on the back. Handwrite the address and the note. Make it look personal. But make sure you print clearly so they recognize your name. These are great for short notes, thank yous, reminders, and so on.

FOREIGN POST CARDS

When you travel — whether for business or a vacation — send post cards to your clients and prospects. Again, handwrite the address and the note so it looks personal. Keep it simple: "Business is booming here." Send as many as you can. You might even arrange with someone from the locale to buy the postcards before you go and send them to you in bulk. Then you can write them out before you fly and as you fly, and when you arrive you can just mail them and you're done.

A post card is a personal touch. Choose attractive cards that people might put up in their office. They will remember that you thought to send them post cards from Europe, Asia, the Rockies, the East Coast, the islands, Disney World . . .

Don't wait for travel to foreign lands. You can mail post cards from different regions of your own country.

CUSTOM-PRINTED POST CARDS

Print your own post cards. You might use a quotation, a catchy phrase, a product photo, an illustration, or a cartoon. If you have a book, the post card can be modelled after the book cover. Make the card something people will keep and show to others. Don't make it just an ad, although it's fine to print your ad on the back. The front should catch their attention.

Your custom cards could be printed in full colour or black and white. Colours will cost more, although you can get a one-colour card almost as cheaply as one in black and white. You can also add colour relatively inexpensively by using coloured paper.

Because the costs drop dramatically for large quantities, consider collaborating with colleagues to print a joint promotional post card.

Here are some examples of post cards I have used.

This works because Bill Cosby is universally liked — and it is good advice.

This card was popular because it expressed a simple truth, one that everyone has learned the hard way. It means something different to everyone, yet all identify with it.

GIFTS

Gifts are relationship builders, not bribes. There's no need to give a contact a new car or Mediterranean cruise. Gifts should never place obligations on the receiver. It's inappropriate to sniff and say, "Well, after I sent you those game tickets I thought you would do business with me." It just doesn't work that way.

Gifts are given as a thank you for past business and opportunities or as a "thinking of you" memento. The purpose of the gift is to remind the recipient of you and to make them feel good. The more unique your gift,

Buy Gifts — Cards-x-mas

the more powerful and memorable it is. It helps if the gifts say something about you, as in the story below.

SPECIAL GIFTS

My North American clients know that I am Swiss because of my accent, so I flaunt it. Each time I visit Switzerland, I buy Swiss chocolate for some of my top clients. Rather than mail them from there (it would cost a lot more and they might spoil in transit), I send them out when I return home, each one with a handwritten "post-it" greeting.

Very few people don't love Swiss chocolate. And do they remember me? Oh, yes!

— *PETER*

LETTERS

If you must type letters, personalize them by adding a handwritten postscript or highlighting important points with a highlighter. Most people read the postscript first, so make sure that's where you put your most important point. Have another important point? Add a P.P.S.

When typing the name and address, always format the person's name in boldface type, in a slightly larger font than you use for the rest of the letter. That helps the name jump off the page and catch the reader's attention.

Never address a letter "To whom it may concern." And sending a letter to a title without a name is equivalent to addressing it to "Occupant." Call and get the name. You don't build relationships with titles — you build them with people. Everyone's favourite sound is the sound of their own name.

When making a new contact should you call first or send mail first?

Call first. Get the name. Talk to the person. Ask them if they would like the information. Then do as promised and send it. That way they may remember your name, and may even be looking for your mailing when it arrives. Information that arrives without warning is considered junk mail, and often lands unopened in the round file.

POST-IT NOTES

Use post-it notes to further personalize your mailing. Attach them throughout the documents you send to emphasize key points and guide the recipient through the material. Use a colour that stands out from the mailing. Yellow post-it notes are usually best.

CUSTOM-PRINTED POST-IT NOTES

Better still, print your own post-it notes with your name and phone number, and perhaps the name of your product line. Write their first name on the note, add a short message, and sign your name. You can send pads of these notes to your clients. They'll use them in their own work, and your name will always be top-of-mind.

PERSONAL MASS MAIL

I received a mailing containing a page torn from a magazine and a post-it note attached, with a note to me saying, "Geo, This looks good. — B." It was a nice touch. They get A for effort. But they made a few errors.

First, what they did well: The page looked like it had been torn from a magazine. That is a nice personal touch. I was inclined to think, "Someone cared enough to carefully rip this from their magazine and send it to me."

Second, there was a post-it note with what appeared to be handwriting addressed to me. On closer examination I noticed the handwriting was mass-produced in blue to make it look authentic.

Where they erred: The note was signed "B." Who the heck is "B"? Even if it was signed "Bob," that still didn't tell me anything. It turned out there was nothing personal about that note — in fact, it actually annoyed me. If you are personalizing a message, always write your full name clearly. You want them to know who it is, and not mistake you for some other Bob.

The note was addressed to "Geo," a short-form of George. I don't like it. That also annoyed me. The article was not clear. That frustrated me. It wasn't clear who the company was or what it was

about. It might have been one of those multi-level marketing schemes for all I knew. There was a number to call.

I did not call, and it went into the garbage.

— GEORGE (NOT GEO!)

FAXES

It didn't take long for junk fax to become commonplace. Be careful of broadcast faxing, because it really is considered junk mail. Faxing can be timely but impersonal. If you must send broadcast faxes, use them to make short announcements, and keep them to one page in length. Faxing may be much cheaper than paper mail, but it's much less effective.

The one area where broadcast faxes seem to work well is for association newsletters or announcements of upcoming events.

When you send faxes, make them personal by attaching a post-it note to the fax sheet and handwriting the person's name. If you want your fax to be noticed in the pile, use very large type and use few words.

PHONE CALLS

You can't get much more personal than with a real conversation. Stay in touch with your contacts by making a quick call to find out what has changed: Has she had a promotion? Does he have a new boss, new owners, a new address? Call with a reason. Have one key question or new information. Always introduce yourself fully, giving your first and last name. If you have interrupted them, it might take a few seconds for them to focus on the call. See the sections on "Voice mail" (Chapter 1) and "Cold calling" (Chapter 5) for some tips on handling these kinds of calls.

E-MAIL

This is a great way to stay in contact with your clients and colleagues. It is personal, timely, virtually cost-free, and it gets read. Send and read your e-mail outside of normal business hours. Include your signature (identification information about you and your business) at the end of your e-mail messages. Your signature should list your name, phone and fax numbers, address, and a statement of what you do. See Chapter 3 for more information on e-mail messaging.

2.2 NETWORKING

Dig your well before you're thirsty.
— HARVEY MACKAY

NETWORKING: FIVE MYTHS AND REALITIES

Networking has a bad name. Ever visit one of those networking meetings? You're told, "Arrive with a pocketful of business cards and don't leave until they're all gone." I get so desperate to escape that I stuff the free gift box with a fistful of my cards and take off!

MYTH #1: YOU MUST GIVE YOUR CARD TO EVERYONE IN THE ROOM.

If people aren't interested they won't keep your card, let alone call you.
Reality: It is more important to get business cards than to hand them out.
After you identify a prospect, ask for their card. Mark which ones are important. When you have their card, *you* control the contact. Add them to your database and follow up.

MYTH #2: NETWORKING IS SELLING.

The term *network marketing* confuses people. It is meant to. Network marketing, also known as MLM, or Multi-Level Marketing, generates sales through a vast, layered network of product representatives, each of whom is given incentive to recruit still more committed reps. MLM sales pitches can come across as vague and evasive.
Reality: Networking is marketing.
When you network you are building a network — hence the term — of people who know about you and your product. They may buy from you or help you. Networking is a long-term strategy, not a quick-sell scheme.

MYTH #3: NETWORKING IS TELLING YOUR STORY.

Watch out for Power Networkers, who, full of bluster, talk *at* you. They condescend and announce, in effect, "You must be stupid not to buy my product. If you order now, you'll get the network special discount."
Reality: Networking is communicating.
Listen more than you talk. Remember the simple formula: two ears, one

Nuts your network — it will grow.

mouth. Use them in proportion. Get your message into a 30-second format. Open with a question, appeal to your listeners' self-interest, and end with a call to action. When you talk, observe their interest level. When their eyes glaze over, it's time to move along. Thank them and walk away. But if they show interest, ask them questions. "Do you see a way that this service might help you or someone you know?" Ask about their business, their most nagging problem, their greatest achievement, their next challenge, their best advice, or their newest idea. Listen to the answers. You learn more by listening.

MYTH #4: NETWORKING ENDS WHEN YOU WALK OUT THE DOOR.
Reality: Networking is about building and maintaining relationships.
Record the names in your database. Follow up with a phone call, an e-mail message, regular mail, or a meeting over coffee or lunch. Maintain your contacts.

MYTH #5: SEND THEM INFORMATION ONLY ABOUT YOUR PRODUCT.
If all you do is mail brochures, then all you are doing is advertising. It's okay to advertise, and a mailing list is good; but a mailing list is not a network. If you want to build a relationship, you must send something of value.
Reality: A network is built by sharing something of value.
The fuel that keeps a network alive is helpfulness. How do you help people? If you listen, you will discover their interests. Send them an article that might interest them, recommend a book, compliment them when they do something wonderful — or, better still, give them a hot lead. It's okay to send them your brochure, but do more than that. Most importantly, do these things without expecting tit-for-tat. If you nurture your network and help others, eventually you will reap your rewards.

REMEMBER THE BAMBOO
Networking is like planting bamboo. You seldom see immediate benefits. When you plant and cultivate bamboo, you do a lot of work for the first seven years, but see little growth. Bamboo only grows about twelve inches — in seven years! Then after the seventh year

100

they shoot up to be six feet tall.

Imagine if bamboo farmers gave up in the seventh year — or before. Networking is about waiting for relationships to grow — it takes time.

2.3 RELATIONSHIPS WITH GROUPS

So far I have talked about building personal relationships with individuals. These are the strongest relationships. But what about having relationships with groups? No, I don't mean relationships à la Hugh Hefner. You want to develop relationships with groups because individual people belong to groups and the individual person is whom you ultimately want to reach.

If you recognize the groups that people around you fall into, then you are ready to develop individual approaches for each group. Working through groups multiplies your reach. Designing personal approaches to each group strengthens the relationship. Categorizing people into groups also makes it easier to manage your database. See Chapter 5 for details on creating and maintaining your database.

If you think about it, you will realize that I have been talking about three key groups so far — clients, prospects, and media. In each case, you must design an approach for the group, then continue to personalize that contact for individual members.

You might not think of clients as a group because they never get together to meet and discuss you. If they did, you might get a little worried. Even though you might design a common approach to your client group, you never want them to get the idea that you think of them as part of a group. They must think that you see them as a unique client. Never send out a letter addressed "Dear Clients." The same applies to prospects and media. See Chapter 3 for an in-depth discussion of the media in all its forms.

In the next few pages you will read about groups that you can take a more "group" approach with. For example, you will not offend if you send out a notice addressed "Dear Staff," "Dear Suppliers," or "Dear Association

Members." Make the relationship as personal as you can, but in the end these groups don't mind being thought of as groups.

Beware that groups, like companies, take on a personality or culture of their own — especially large or long-established groups. If you want groups to think well and speak well of you, you must think and speak well of them. A group may be good even if there are some bad people in it. So never write off a group after a bad experience with a few individual members.

Before we discuss the individual types of groups, keep in mind that staff, suppliers, and competitors have the potential to have the biggest impact on your business. Treat them well. Associates and alliances should be chosen and created very carefully, to best suit your needs. And other groups can't be changed, but you can choose which ones to join and work with: networking and lead generators; service clubs; alumni associations; and professional associations.

STAFF

Recruit your full- and part-time staff as marketers. Make them feel good about you, your company, and your product. Let them know that marketing is the responsibility of everyone in the company. Help them understand what you do and how you differ from the competition. Hang a sign on the wall that states your company purpose. Introduce your staff to clients and suppliers. Be proud of them and they will be proud of you. Honour your employees with awards. Give each of them their own business cards. It is a small expense, but one that makes them feel they belong. Teach them to listen to clients and prospects.

SUPPLIERS

Recruit your suppliers as marketers. Be firm with them, but never nasty: demand good pricing, but treat them fairly and consistently. Pay them on time. If you're late with your payments they'll think that either your business is bad, or you are neglectful and even mean. If you treat them fairly, they will help you when you are in a pinch.

Make sure your suppliers know what you do and what is important to your clients. Recommend them to others, and they will recommend you. Ask them to put up your card or flyer in their shop. Do a joint promotion with them. Share coffee and exchange some ideas.

Get your banker on your side. Send your materials from time to time. Call them just to talk and meet for coffee occasionally. You will stand out in their mind. When you need financial help they are more likely to be of assistance. They may recommend you when they hear of bargains or business opportunities.

Get all your business and personal suppliers on side: your lawyer, accountant, printer, dentist, hairdresser, and so on.

Establish relationships with a small number of suppliers and then deal with them regularly. Build a mutually beneficial relationship. Show and tell them what you do and ask for ideas. It is a great source of free consulting.

When ordering supplies or services, explain what you need. Then ask for their suggestions on how to have more impact, save on costs, or save time. If you ask for advice, they will likely offer it and help you. Don't tell them how to do their job. Remember that they are experts at what they do — harness that expertise. Make them feel like partners by working with them instead of abusing them.

ASSOCIATES AND ALLIANCES

Create a formal or informal associate relationship with other people or enterprises. You could come together as a kind of virtual corporation to tackle a particular project, then disband at the close of the project. This kind of arrangement is particularly helpful if your service is a specialized task in what is usually a more involved project. In order to get a particular job you may need to be a general contractor and pull in your associates. If you give the alliance a name (e.g., "Me and Associates") you can have a common logo and get alliance business cards and stationery.

Here's an example. Imagine you are a computer programmer and the client needs a system redesign. You may need to bring in an analyst, project manager, network specialist, job practice consultant, and trainer.

You can do joint promotions, exchange leads, and cover for each other. Some alliances share office space to split the cost.

With associates, you appear bigger than you are. You can take on bigger jobs. And from working with these associates you will learn their strengths and feel comfortable referring other business to each other. Pick your associates carefully — you are judged by whom you associate with.

COMPETITORS

Treat your competitors with the respect they deserve. Remember, what goes around comes around.

Know what your competitors charge for their services. Then when you talk to prospects and discover who they used or are using, you know their budget range. You learn whether you are too expensive or too cheap for their perception of value. If prospects are used to paying $1,000 and you offer your service for $500, they will think you are not very good. But if they are unhappy with the quality of a $1,000 supplier, they might be shopping for a $2,000 supplier.

Learn about your competition by talking with them, examining their literature, and reading about them in the media. Also learn about your competition by querying your prospects. When you find a prospect happy with their existing supplier, ask, "What is it that most impresses you with this supplier?" Then listen carefully to the answer. You might follow with, "Why is this benefit so important to you?" Add, "Are there other needs you have that are not being met by this supplier?"

If you specialize in Macintosh computers, you can exchange referrals with a PC specialist. You help each other — and you help your clients, who also discover that you have their interests in mind. You are not trying to hog all the business. If you are too busy to take on a job, you might refer business to a competitor. Just make sure you recommend someone who will make the client happy. If you discover that a prospect's budget is much lower than your rate, recommend a junior competitor who is within their price range. On the other hand, if the scope of the work is beyond your capability, recommend a more developed competitor, or partner with that competitor on this project.

Your competition should also know about you. Send them some of your information, especially when you are featured in the media. They may not like you, but they will respect you. And when they are asked about you, they can answer, "Oh, yes, we have heard of her."

NETWORKING AND LEAD-GENERATION GROUPS

These groups exist to share prospect leads between colleagues in different businesses. For example, a real estate salesperson might advise a mover about a client who just sold a house. A car salesperson might tell a car insurance sales agent about a client who just bought a new car. A hairdresser might share leads on all kinds of information they learn from their clients.

Because these groups usually limit membership to only one person per category, you will not have direct competition within the group. So if you are a landscaper, all landscape inquiries come to you.

When you attend the meetings you get a chance to stand and present a 30-second commercial to the other members of your group. Remember to hone your 30-second message (see pages 58–59).

SERVICE CLUBS

Here are a few of the better-known service clubs: Rotary, Lions, Lionesses, Optimists, Kinsmen, Kinettes, and Kiwanis. They are trustworthy organizations that raise money for community projects. Don't join thinking you will get a lot of business. Join only if you are prepared to get involved as a volunteer in community projects. Along the way you will develop great relationships with other members of your community. They will learn more about your character, which is good in the long run for your business. Service clubs require a lot of time and commitment.

ALUMNI ASSOCIATIONS

Stay in touch with your college or university alumni association. Stay on the mailing list. Attend some of the special events — luncheons, golf days, speaker series, etc. It is always worthwhile getting involved on the board. The funny thing about alumni is that they often feel a special bond with each other, even if they attended the school in entirely differently decades.

For this reason it is very good to get published in the alumni newsletter or magazine. They typically devote a section to reporting what alumni are doing and where they work. Check out your alumni Hall of Fame for key contacts, prospects, or mentors. See Chapters 1 and 3 of this book for information on getting published.

Join some associations

When you get the chance, go to your high school reunion. (Don't forget to take your business cards.) Sometimes high school bonds are even stronger than those forged in university.

You might include your alma mater in your bio when you publish an article or book or make a speech. Fellow graduates will often approach you to acknowledge the connection.

> I don't want to join the kind of club
> that accepts people like me as members.
> — GROUCHO MARX

PROFESSIONAL ASSOCIATIONS

If you join the association for the field you are in, it's easy to stay in touch with the latest developments and maintain contact with your competition and potential partners.

Associations are always looking for board volunteers. Being on the board is a great way to gain the respect of your peers. As a board member it is easier to meet the members. And you start relationships with a certain built-in level of respect. President is the most prestigious position on any board, but I recommend you be in charge of public relations. Why? Because as official spokesperson for the association, you can develop a relationship with the media. The media and the public will see your name on announcements from the association and assume you are an expert in your field.

You get a greater value from your activity as public relations person. Every time you send out information, you are also sending out your name. If you are creative and do some effective promotion for the association, your fellow board members will love you, because you're making the whole board look good. The association members feel good that their association has received notice in the media, and they remember that you were responsible.

Later, when you send your own business information to the media, they will recognize your name and associate you with the respect they hold for the association. Your clients will see your name in a prestigious role and feel good about doing business with you.

> Do not protect yourself by a fence, but rather by your friends.
> — CZECH PROVERB

2.4 SPECIAL RELATIONSHIPS

FAMILY

Your family may be involved directly in your business. If you can make that work it is a major accomplishment. You should be proud. But even if they're not directly involved, they can be part of your marketing efforts. They probably believe in you more than anyone else does, so it's only natural that they would be your best marketers. Don't expect them to do anything, but just in case, keep them informed. Then when they come through for you, shower them with appreciation.

Teach your family your purpose statement. Describe your ideal customers. Tell them what you really do well. They each have a network of friends and acquaintances that is different from yours, and they could spread the word, whether that means your child talks about you for "Show & Tell" or your spouse introduces you at his or her office party. Even your in-laws might brag about your business — but not in front of you of course.

> I'm gonna make him an offer he can't refuse.
> — DON CORLEONE OF THE GODFATHER
> *AS HE PROMISES TO HELP HIS GODSON GET AN IMPORTANT JOB*

Talking about family is a great way to connect with others, because we all have family. Just casually mentioning my teenagers is enough to get clients offering me advice — and condolences. If they have younger children, I remind them how cute they are now, and warn them to "Enjoy them while you can." We have a good laugh and they feel good about their family.

> Ask the experienced rather than the learned.
> — ARABIC PROVERB

John Muro-mentor

MENTORS

Find a mentor. Mentors can help you cut years off your growth curve, and they will prevent you from making mistakes that they have already made or seen others make. This leaves you free to learn from new mistakes.

A mentor is someone — perhaps a family member, friend, or business associate — who is more experienced in the business and who is willing to give you some of their time, advice, and support. Mentors never do this for money. They enter into the relationship because they want to help you. They see some potential in you and maybe a little of themselves in you. They want to help and you must be ready.

Besides the advice and coaching, they can help you by opening doors — that is, by allowing you to use their name, or by introducing you to key contacts. They may include you in one of their projects, refer overflow business to you, or drop your name in conversations.

HOW TO FIND A MENTOR

Just because you need a mentor does not mean you will find one. You must adopt a marketing approach to finding a mentor. Get out to business functions, get known in your community, associations, clubs, and industry. Watch the news for potential mentors; send them notes, thank yous, and congratulations. Call them to meet for breakfast or coffee.

HOW TO MAINTAIN A MENTORING RELATIONSHIP

Respect their time, advice, and experience. Ask them probing questions and listen — taking notes is good. Ask what three things they would do differently if they were starting over. Ask about the three smartest things they ever did — then try to do them. Ask about their biggest obstacles and how they overcame them. Ask about their dumbest mistakes. Learn from their mistakes. Ask what they wish someone had told them when they started.

Ask a lot, but take what is offered.
— *RUSSIAN PROVERB*

Ask questions, listen, and then act on what you learn. Report back with the results, even if they weren't great. At least you listened and tried.

That's what they want to hear. Never blame them if it doesn't work. On the other hand, give them credit for the successes. You get some credit for implementing their suggestions, but make sure you express your appreciation and respect.

Thank them for their help — and be sincere.
Never waste their time.
Give back to them, with your ideas, thoughts, and help.

A mentoring relationship can end for any of the following reasons:

- You outgrow the mentor.
- You waste the mentor's time.
- The chemistry goes out of the relationship.
- The mentor puts you down instead of helping you up.
- You lose respect for each other.

The worst thing you can do to a mentor is ask for their advice and then ignore it. Use what you learn from them. Try it, even if you put your own spin on it.

Be not afraid of growing slowly; be afraid of standing still.
— CHINESE PROVERB

COMMUNITY AND BUSINESS LEADERS

Whom you know is important. Even more important is who knows you. Watch your local news. Look for opportunities to call or send a note of congratulations to the local leaders. Call and invite them to lunch or coffee. You are building relationships that will pay off in the long term. (One may even turn into a mentoring relationship.) Don't spend their time yapping about how good you are. Instead, ask about them and listen. Then they will know you are good. Keep them informed about what you are doing. But make it matter-of-fact; don't turn it into a sales pitch.

The more we see you hanging around with leaders — the more we will think of you as a leader.

MORE RELATIONSHIP TIPS

To reach VIPs, establish relationships with their secretaries, receptionists, administrative assistants, chauffeurs, etc.

Learn memory techniques to remember names — people will love you.

If you send people birthday greetings — they will love you.

Read a broad range of topics. That makes it easier to carry on a conversation and relate to different people.

Listen to other people's plans or problems and ask later how they turned out.

Send gifts that people can share with their spouses.

SOME FINAL THOUGHTS ON RELATIONSHIPS

Relationships need to be fed to stay alive. Don't call after ten years and act like you are old buddies.

Stay in touch regularly but don't be a pest.

Be consistent with your message and style. Coke keeps sending the same message.

Be unique to stay remembered. Stand out from the crowd.

Be yourself — not a fake. If they ran into you somewhere, would they recognize you?

Be persistent. Remember the bamboo tree.

If you are already practising some of these principles — keep doing it.

If you are not — start now and make it a habit.

> Chains of habit are too light to be felt
> until they are too heavy to be broken.
> — *WARREN BUFFETT*

Relationship-Building Action List

☐ Call regularly
☐ Call when you have news of an opportunity that might interest them
☐ Return calls quickly
☐ Send notes

- ❐ Send thank yous
- ❐ Send congratulations
- ❐ Send post cards
- ❐ Send articles you've written
- ❐ Send articles of interest to them
- ❐ Send articles about them/their industry/about their competition
- ❐ Send your book
- ❐ Send a book you think they will love
- ❐ Recommend a book you just read
- ❐ Send a cartoon/quotation/funny story
- ❐ Send notice of your speaking engagement
- ❐ Send notice of a special event
- ❐ Send tickets for a special event
- ❐ Send information about an interesting seminar or conference
- ❐ Send copies of your news release
- ❐ Send a special gift
- ❐ Send your newsletter
- ❐ Send your new product news
- ❐ Meet for breakfast/coffee/lunch
- ❐ Send a free product sample
- ❐ Recommend a supplier to them
- ❐ Refer a lead to them
- ❐ Introduce them to a good contact
- ❐ Visit their web site and comment on it
- ❐ Visit their booth at the trade show
- ❐ Apologize when you make an error
- ❐ Ask their advice
- ❐ Help them with a problem
- ❐ Warn them of a potential problem

> Dear Lord, if the world is overpopulated,
> how come no one ever comes to visit me?
> — BEN WICKS CARTOON

SUMMARY
SECRETS OF RELATIONSHIPS

- Build and nurture relationships with those who are like you. Connect with others who have common backgrounds, likes, hobbies, family activities, culture.

- Create and maintain personal relationships. Say "thank you" often. Say it with handwritten notes, post cards, e-mail, by phone, with a book, with a gift, or with official recognition.

- Plant your bamboo — then cultivate with care, persistence, and patience. It takes time. Networks are built by helping others.

- Harness your staff, suppliers, and colleagues. Know your competition and get them to know about you. Visit your alumni association events. Join your professional association.

- Associate with others who improve your credibility — associates, partners, mentors, community leaders, and business executives.

A good, solid reputation is built over a lifetime.
But the power of the media can make you
a hero or a zero in no time!
— Peter Urs Bender

Media

**Facing the media
is more difficult than bathing a leper.**
— *Mother Teresa*

STRATEGY THREE

The media are extremely effective marketing tools. When you think of the media, the first thing that comes to mind might be advertising. Beware of advertising — it is the most expensive form of media exposure and the least effective. Instead, try to be seen in the media as an expert.

Compile a list of media contacts. Maintain it. You will need to update it as names change and people move around, and when new publications are launched and others die. Keep your eyes peeled for publications when you visit the bookstore, conference centres, malls, hotels, and the lobbies of your clients' business offices. Jot down the publication name, address, phone numbers, contact names, and e-mail addresses — or just take the publication with you. Take special note of what your clients read. Those are the publications in which you would prefer to appear.

It's better to have the media say negative things about you than to not be featured at all. Any publicity is better than none. Most people don't read all the details; and many forget. If they liked you before the bad news, they'll continue to like you once the dust has cleared.

Try to turn the negative into a positive. If *Time* magazine says something bad about you, you're perfectly entitled to use this in your résumé: "Appeared in *Time* magazine." It looks impressive when you list in your portfolio the publications in which you have appeared.

Disguise yourself's as News

There are three ways to appear in the media, as shown in the following chart. Each kind of appearance has its advantages and disadvantages. Naturally, it is ideal if you can get the media to write about you positively, to quote you, or to feature you as a guest or news story.

	Cost	**Credibility**	**Control of Content**
Advertising	Most	Least	Most
A direct appearance: you write or speak	↑	↓	↑
Media talk about you	Least	Most	Least

MEDIA ATTENTION

Media attention is like money: if you don't have any, you need it badly, and nobody gives it to you. As soon as you have some (or a lot), everybody wants to give you more.

To get some exposure, you have to start somewhere. It could be the paper in your neighbourhood or a small trade publication. It doesn't matter where it is, but you have to cultivate some relationships with writers who can tell the public about you.

Media attention won't just come from heaven. Nobody will phone you. You are your own media agency. Go to them.

ADVERTISING

Try to avoid paid advertising. Everyone recognizes ads and discounts them as less credible than other types of exposure. If you must pay for an ad, design it so that it doesn't look like one. Make it an "advertorial," or a print tool that presents information in an article format. The publication that carries your advertorial will probably label it with the words "advertorial" or "paid advertising" to make it clear that it is separate from their own editorial content. Negotiate to have them use the word "advertorial"; it is much more effective than "paid advertising." Some publications may disguise this type of advertisement by calling it a "corporate profile" or "business spotlight." If you must advertise, disguise it as news.

When negotiating the purchase of advertising, think like a tough customer. You might have to talk to their competition to get a better deal.

If you advertise in one of your customers' trade publications, make sure you're listed as a sponsor instead of as an advertiser. A sponsor seems friendlier than an advertiser. The perception is that we believe a sponsor is supporting us, while an advertiser just wants to sell us something.

Sponsor events, publications, and awards for the associations that your customers belong to.

SYNERGY IN THE MEDIA

The more the media talks about you, the more other media will talk about you. The more frequently you appear, the more the market notices. The more they notice, the more they *see* you. The more you are seen, the more they want you.

BUILDING RELATIONSHIPS WITH THE MEDIA

Find your favourite writers, editors, and columnists. If you like their style, it's probably because they are like you in some way. They may like you for the same reasons you like them.

Think of your relationship with the media as special. Everything that you would do to build relationships with key clients and prospects goes double for the media. Send them notes, post cards, and information.

THE BEST WAY TO GET THE ATTENTION OF THE NEWS MEDIA:
Send food.

Don't send groceries — send special food.

No bacon and eggs — send treats, chocolate, desserts, fruit, cheese and crackers . . .

Use the food to mark special occasions: the recipient's anniversary, your anniversary, new product launches, and so on. Work with a specialty treat shop to customize the food to your logo or theme.

Always be honest with the media. Don't pretend to be the expert you are not. If they call you and you are not the right fit for their spot, decline and recommend someone else. They will appreciate your honesty and call you another time.

Tell them the truth, first because it is the right thing to do
and second because they'll find out anyway.
— PAUL GALVIN, CEO MOTOROLA DURING THE 1930S
(AFTER BEING ASKED TO MISREPRESENT THEIR ROUGH TIMES TO THE MEDIA)

In 1982, Johnson & Johnson pulled Tylenol from store shelves after capsules were found to be poisoned. The move put customer safety before profit, and CEO Jim Burke set a new standard for media openness.

FORMS OF MEDIA

You have a wide range of media at your disposal. First there were newspapers, then radio, then television, and now there's the Internet. As technology introduces new forms of media, each with a different kind of impact, you must be aware of the opportunities they represent. Maximize your marketing reach by seizing these opportunities.

Media Type	Senses Used	Means of Communication
Traditional		
Print	visual	text, still images
Radio	auditory	sound and spoken words
Television	visual and auditory	sound, text, spoken words, still and moving images
New		
Internet	visual and auditory	sound, text, spoken words, still and moving images

Later in this chapter, you'll learn how to use each of these types of media to your advantage, but keep this in mind: Of all forms of media available to you, print is where you want to be, because it is permanent. Radio can be great because it reaches listeners in their cars on the daily commute, but as on television, your radio appearance happens at a certain moment in time and then it's gone. You can tell people that you appeared on radio and television, but if they didn't see the broadcast, how can they ever be sure? With print media, you can remove all doubt by sending them a copy of the article that mentioned or featured you.

This doesn't mean you should give up on radio and television — they can sometimes result in a tremendous boost to credibility and sales. Their effectiveness depends on the audience of the show and the timing. For example, having your book mentioned on Oprah will practically guarantee sales of a million copies — if you have the stock and a good distribution system.

> You are not heard on radio — until they know you.
> You are not seen on television — until they recognize you.
> But if you are in print — you can always send them a copy.

A Word About Your Own Media

You can always create your own media, so you have complete control over content and distribution. But because your own media will have less credibility than traditional outlets, you must design them to inform rather than persuade. If your chosen media just become pure advertising vehicles, your clients will not read them unless they are in the middle of making a buying decision. Your homemade media must provide value in the form of entertainment or information that readers or viewers can use. Your own media might include:

* newsletter
* column
* book
* your own radio or TV show
* web site
* tapes
* CDs

3.1 NEWS RELEASES

News releases are used by large corporations, governments, associations, public relations agencies, and small businesses as their most direct and fundamental tool for communicating with the media. And no wonder: in

1980, *Wall Street Journal* executive editor Frederick Taylor admitted that as much as 90 percent of the *Journal*'s daily news originated in self-interested press releases. For this reason, you should make the news release an important plank in your marketing program. If the media is always talking about you, there is little need for expensive advertising. You can help the media talk about you, and influence how they talk about you, through your news releases. You cannot control the media. All you can do is attempt to establish and maintain open communication. They report the news as they see it. You can try to be part of the news, but you do not have the *right* to be part of the news.

Start with a goal of sending out one news release every month. Depending on your market you might choose to send them out more or less frequently. Once you've set the target, look for items of information you think the media might find interesting. This isn't as difficult as it may seem; you can simply tell the media about something that *might happen, will happen,* or *already happened.* As concrete examples, here are three key reasons to send out a news release: to preview or review an event, to announce an award, or to provide information. Consider the following suggestions, and add your own ideas to the lists:

1. *Event* (You may send a news release both *before* and *after* an event.)
   Launch of a new business
   Opening of a new office/store/plant
   Anniversary of a product/business/direction/location
   Appointment of a new CEO/staff/directors
   Launch of a new service/product line
   Sales milestone — tenth project, 100 clients, $1 million in sales
   Signing of a big contract
   Welcoming of a new owner/partner/investor
   Development of new technology
   Acquisition of international partner/project
   Open house/tour
   Speaking engagement
   Information seminar

2. *Award/acknowledgement* (Let the media know when you or your business are noted for any of the following achievements or activities.)

You receive a professional/academic designation or certification

You are honoured or elected by an association

You receive a community award

You sponsor a community award/cause/charity

You sponsor a contest

You receive a business award

You present an award

You give away a prize

You are recognized as an approved supplier

3. *Information* (What useful information can you provide to the marketplace?)

Results of a survey

Advice on a common problem

Interesting facts about or trends in the industry

Market indicators

Seasonal facts

Predictions

Safety/health warnings

Tips lists

} Media
} Vehicle

HOW TO WRITE A NEWS RELEASE

FORMAT

Don't be afraid to call it a "news release." You could also call it a "news bulletin" or "announcement," but avoid the term "press release" — it sounds like propaganda.

For perspective, always lead off with the city and date of release. Then add the statement "For Immediate Use." This implies urgency. It also allows the media some choice on when to run it. If the news is date-sensitive, indicate whether it is "For use before ___" or "For use after ___."

One glance at your release should reveal who sent it, that is, your company name or your organization. If you have a logo, use it.

Should you fax or mail your news release? If it's urgent, use the fax.

But to get noticed, mail it. The media receive a lot of "junk" faxes, and they all look alike. If you mail your message you have a better chance of attracting attention with the colour and feel of the paper you choose. Use high-quality paper. You may want to use your letterhead if it works with the design of the message you're sending. Attach post-it notes addressed to the person you want to reach. Handwrite the address on the envelope.

You might get lucky sending your release to the "newsroom" or "editor." But you will have much better luck addressing it to an individual. Which do you read first — letters marked "occupant" or those with your name on it? The media are made up of people too.

Make your bulletin easy to read and short — one page maximum. Use a good-sized font; twelve-point works well. Add a little spice by printing key names in boldface, but sprinkle lightly. Italic type draws attention, but it's hard to read. Make sure you use upper- and lower-case type. IT IS EXTREMELY DIFFICULT TO READ TYPE PRINTED ENTIRELY IN CAPITAL LETTERS. Use many short paragraphs and short sentences. Double spacing is always best.

At the bottom of the page, write "End" or "– 30 –" or "# # #." Each is known to indicate the end of a communication.

Show your company's contact name(s) and phone number(s) very clearly at the bottom or top of the page. If you list people besides yourself, make sure they will be available and knowledgeable enough to talk to the press when a call comes in. Impress on those contacts the idea that the media require speedy responses to make their deadlines. Each of your company's internal contacts should have copies of the news release and be prepared to answer questions with authority and credibility.

CONTENT

Start with a strong title. A subtitle is not necessary if the title is strong. Study newspaper headlines for ideas, or examine the style adopted by your target media.

You have only one chance to hook them with the title. If you fail to grab them, they will not read any further. Remember, the media will probably preview the release with one glance at your headline. Your title must include words, themes, companies, personalities, or issues that slow their eyes and invite them to read the first paragraph.

The first sentence must seize their interest. Rework that first sentence until the first few words (or even the first word) pull the reader in.

The first paragraph is crucial. If your media contacts read that far, they are likely to be drawn right into the story. Think of it this way: if they were to print only one paragraph, it would probably be your first one, so write it to contain your most important message. Don't keep them guessing — you are not writing a mystery novel.

Write the most important message first, then follow with the next points in order of decreasing importance. Assume that they might chop it after any paragraph. Write each paragraph applying the same approach to your sentences: if they only print a single sentence, it would be the first one.

Good news releases are not written, they are rewritten and rewritten. Each time you revise yours, think chop, chop, chop. If you can't fit it all on one page, then chop, chop, chop.

Proofread *before* you send out your release. Journalists are especially sensitive to poor grammar and typos. It hurts them to read garbage — so they'll just toss it instead.

The media will read your release thinking, "Will this interest my readers, listeners, or viewers, and is it unique?" It doesn't have to be wildly unique — just a little special. Every January we get news about the first baby born in the New Year, because the first one is unique at that time. The second is not news.

Relate the news to the reader. Why is it important to the media's readers, listeners, or viewers? Test for significance by asking yourself, "So what?"

In your copy, answer a reporter's key questions: who, what, why, where, when, and how. You could even use these questions as subheadings, or as a summary. They are also good for testing the quality of your message before you send it out.

Quotations are always interesting to the media. You might use quotations from company officials, community leaders, or customers. When you use a name, always state the person's position (e.g., CEO, National Sales Manager, President and Founder, author of ___). Use quotations that evoke emotion, create controversy, or present a position.

You can use a quotation to make a statement that you could not make yourself. For example, it's fair to write, "According to Lee Brown, 'This company is the best value for money in the country.'" You couldn't state the quoted material as a fact because it may not be true, and it is difficult to substantiate. The media will not print something that might not be true or might land them in hot water for misrepresentation or libel; but they *will* print an attributed opinion. For example, the media might print "'He is a crook,' charged Lee Brown." However, they would not print "He is a crook." The first is reporting an opinion; the second statement might be libelous.

When your news is about people, don't introduce too many new names in one release. This confuses readers. Talk about one or two.

When you do use a name, write the name in full at first mention. After that you can use only the last name. If you want a name to be remembered, use it several times in the release.

If you are only sending out a few news releases at once, you may wish to slightly customize each release to better grab the specific journalists you are targeting. Try to hit their hot buttons. You'll have to read some of their work to find out what those are.

> And for the tourist who really wants to
> get away from it all, safaris in Vietnam
> — NEWSWEEK *PREDICTING HOLIDAY SPOTS FOR THE 1960s*

TIMING

When you're planning your release, take into account special occasions such as elections and holidays. These change normal news patterns. Trying to get noticed at election time is tough, so don't even bother — unless you have a unique twist on the election issues. If you can spin your news to be relevant to a holiday, you have a better chance of appearing in the news at that time.

Sometimes the media are starving for news. The week between Christmas and the New Year seems to be a slow period. They also may need news in the middle two weeks of August, when many people are on vacation and manufacturers have summer shutdowns. Still others are lying low, preparing to launch their fall stuff in September.

Remember, the news ebbs and flows, depending on what's happening in the world. Your good-news story might end up being pre-empted by an election, a strike, or a disaster. But all is not lost — if your story gets missed and the news is timeless, change the slant and send it another time.

To announce an event, you might want to send a "pre-release" a full month before it's going to take place. Include some highlights to tease the media. Then follow up with the main release and more details two weeks before the event. After the event, send another to tell them what happened. Each release should look different and tell the story from a new viewpoint. Don't send the same thing!

Keep in mind that weekly and monthly publications need more notice than dailies require. Bimonthly and quarterly publications need even more notice.

AFTER THE RELEASE

If your release successfully catches the media's eye, reporters may call for more information or to arrange a photograph. Be available. If you are out of the office, check your voice messages often. The press has short deadlines.

Don't expect to review the reporter's article before publication. You can offer ideas and information but you can't suggest how they should use it. Occasionally they will run the article using the words you chose for your release, but once you give them the information they have control. Reporters may put any spin on it that they wish.

If you send out a news release and receive no response, give the reporter you've targeted a call. But don't call to complain. Ask for some feedback on the news release. First you want to know if it was received on time. Some other questions you might ask include:

Is this type of news of interest to you and your readers?
Should I be contacting someone else at your publication?
Can you tell me why it did not run this time?
What can I do next time to help you use my information?

Is it okay if I send you news of this nature in the future?

Do you have any other suggestions for me?

| Always thank your news contacts for their help.

Keep and file all your news releases in the sequence in which they were sent out — even those that did not elicit any response. Clip and save the articles that ran with the release. Study them to find out what works with whom and when.

I have heard it said that reporters are lazy. I think that may be no more true than in any other profession. They can, however, be overworked, burdened with multiple priorities, pressed by deadlines, and preoccupied with job security concerns or the personal problems that everyone faces.

For these reasons, it is true that the easier you make it for them, the more inclined they are to use your material. Offer them the path of least resistance. Respect their concerns, write good, interesting copy, answer their calls immediately, and treat them as valued clients.

See the next two pages for a sample "pre-release" and news release.

Proud to Be Canadian

2000 Annual Grade 12
Public Speaking Contest

When   Saturday, May 6, 2000
9:00 a.m. sharp — Registration at 8:30 a.m.

Where   Ryerson Polytechnic University
350 Victoria Street, Toronto (one block east of Yonge,
between Gerrard and Dundas, just east of the Eaton Centre)
Mini Theatre A 60

Who   Sponsored by:
Peter Urs Bender
Author of *Secrets of Power Presentations*,
Leadership from Within, and *Secrets of Power Marketing*

Win   First Prize $2,500
Second Prize $1,500
Third Prize $1,000

How   Speech details:
Theme and topic: "Proud to be Canadian"
3 minutes long, use cards, no lectern, no props or visual aids.

Questions and registration:
George Torok
(905) 335-1997; George@Torok.com

Canada's "Presentation Guru" Holds
Fifth Annual Student Public Speaking Contest with Cash Prizes

Toronto, ON — April 9, 2000: Encouraging young people to develop their public speaking skills — and to speak out on why they're Proud to be Canadian — Peter Urs Bender, international speaker and author of the Canadian best-seller *Secrets of Power Presentations*, builds on previous year's success with his fifth annual public speaking contest with cash prizes now totalling $5,000.

The contest, to be held on the morning of Saturday, May 6, 2000, is open to Grade 12 students in the Greater Toronto Area (maximum one student per school, with a total of 25 students), and will take place in Mini Theatre A 60 at Ryerson Polytechnic University, 350 Victoria Street, Toronto. Final speeches will be at 12 noon.

The grand prize–winner will be awarded $2,500; the second prize–winner $1,500; and the third $1,000.

The speech must focus on something positive about Canada and it must be three minutes in length. Interested students should apply through their school principal.

At the age of 23, Swiss-born Peter Urs Bender moved to Canada in 1967 to learn English. Now one of the country's leading speakers, he was selected by Toastmasters International (Ontario) to be the 1995 recipient of its Communication and Leadership Award. Previous recipients include Dr. Roberta Bondar, Mayor Mel Lastman, and former Lieutenant Governor Lincoln Alexander.

Bender is one of only a few Canadians to receive his Certified Speaking Professional (CSP) designation from the National Speakers Association and has been sharing the Secrets of Power Presentations™ for more than a decade. His book — now published in French, German, Indonesian, and Russian — is a practical guide for even the most experienced speaker. Now in its seventh edition, with over 100,000 copies in print, it is required reading in more than 40 Canadian universities and colleges, and is used in many large companies.

– End –

For further information, please contact:
Peter Urs Bender at (416) 491-6690 or George Torok at (905) 335-1997

3.2 PRINT MEDIA

As we've seen, in most cases print media offer the best and most permanent type of exposure. As you prepare to reach out and contact
publications, look beyond the traditional city dailies. All publications
need content. For each of the following, consider how you might
approach them and what they might need for their readers:

- community papers
- daily newspapers
- association newsletters
- association magazines
- trade magazines
- specialized magazines
- special newsletters (investment, cultural, lifestyle)
- company newsletters
- alumni newsletters

And don't forget your own media:

- product and program flyers
- information booklets
- tips sheets
- your newsletter
- your book

When trying to decide where to go first, weigh the effort and return. If it
is very easy to get published in a particular newsletter but there is little
chance of return, do it because the effort was small. If it is difficult to get
published and the market does not seem right, don't bother. However, if
a publication's readers do comprise your target market, keep trying to be
seen in its pages, no matter how tough it is.

Priority	Your clients and prospects . . .	Examples of publications
A	. . . must read the publication.	trade magazines, company newsletters, association newsletters
B	. . . are likely to read the publication.	daily papers, general business, specialty business magazines and newsletters
C	. . . may or may not read the publication — you never know!	hobby, association, community publications, or trade magazines from other fields

WHERE TO START

Start where you are known. That could mean approaching the association of which you are a member. Review its newsletter or magazine. Approach the editor about contributing an article that would be of interest to the readers. As a member you should have a good understanding of relevant issues and your opinion would be valued.

With every article you contribute, ask the editors to print your name, title, company name, city, phone number, e-mail address, and short bio. At the very least, insist on including your name, phone number, and e-mail address!

You might also ask — or even strongly insist — that they print your photo. If the editors tell you it can't be done, gently but firmly repeat your request. I have been successful in getting my photo in publications that had never printed photos before.

Why include your photo? Because many readers will simply skim the publication. If they recognize your photo they will stop and read the article or at least make a mental note that you were the writer. Some will remember that they saw your face somewhere; and when you meet people they will say, "I've heard of you." But they may not be sure where they had seen you before.

> Either write something worth reading
> or do something worth writing.
> — *BENJAMIN FRANKLIN*

The best way to get noticed by the print media is by doing something news-worthy. Then you can accompany that action with news releases. In the best-case scenario, you'll have done something so newsworthy that *the media* call *you* for interviews. Winning a Nobel Prize is one of those achievements.

But let's assume that is not in the plan. Then you have to work for the publicity. If you have established yourself as an expert, they may call you for an opinion. But what else can you do to get noticed? Here are some suggestions:

- write a letter to the editor
- write to a columnist
- write to a reporter
- write to a freelance writer
- write a guest article
- write a regular column
- send a product sample
- send an article
- send your book
- send a report from a third party

If you have targeted a publication as one in which you would like to appear, contact the editor, a columnist, and a reporter. Each may have a different slant and might say yes to your story. They seldom confer with each other. I once organized a special event where the same paper sent two news teams — one from the main office and one from the office of the city where the event was held. Since they were both there, they each submitted stories and both were printed.

Remember that editors and writers are humans, too. They love to get feedback on their work. Send a short note to comment or congratulate them on a well-written article or changes in the publication's format. Some publications rarely receive letters to the editor. If you write short letters to the editor they will love you and print your remarks. They want to encourage others to write.

This is a great way to build a relationship with the media. If you appear to be a source of expert information and opinion they will call you when they need a quote, an expert opinion, or a story.

The national business papers may seem to be the most desirable of all print media, but they are also the most difficult to get into. Contact these papers' writers directly — especially those who write about your industry and your competition. Compliment them on their writing. Tell them how it helped you or how you agree with their advice. Tell them how it applies to your business. Send them some information about your industry. Meet for lunch to talk about business — their business, not yours, unless they ask.

Ask your contacts what information they need and how and when they like to receive it. Depending on their publication frequency, their deadlines may be daily, weekly, monthly, or quarterly. Editors' and writers' lives and temperaments can be mercurial. In the media world, time is everything, so be aware that their moods may change drastically depending on their deadlines.

Unless you are in with the nationals, start with the community paper. Find a friendly contact and ask if the paper's readers would be interested in your idea. Then find out how you should go about submitting an article. The editor will probably give you some guidelines, such as how many words they require, and the newspaper's preferred style. Ask what is more important to them — theory, entertainment, or the application of your idea to the community.

LETTER TO THE EDITOR

This is the easiest way to get published. You don't need to write much; in fact, the shorter your comments, the better. Just state an opinion or clarify a fact.

Make your letter as interesting and controversial as possible. You want people to talk about it. Don't write just to say you enjoyed a particular article. Write to say how that article influenced your actions or how you learned that lesson the hard way or how you strongly disagree because of your extensive research.

Sound controversial but make sure you come across with authority. In other words, sound like the expert. And don't lie.

idea! Ask questions + survey - set addresses + give a prize.

Secrets of Power Marketing

Every publication prints letters to the editor, even if you don't see a letters section. That may just mean that no one has written a letter recently.

How to write a letter to the editor

Decide on how you want to be perceived. What expertise do you have and want to be known for? What opinions do you have and want to be known for?

Scan newspapers, newsletters, and magazines for stories you can

- add to in some way — by giving information or telling a story
- dispute because of your expert opinion
- support with an example
- clarify with more detail or references
- put your own twist on.

Why write to the editor? For one, the editor will get to know you. And more important, your name will appear in print. You can quickly build a portfolio of publications in which you have appeared. You can mention in your résumé the fact that you were published in the national paper — even if your words were in the form of a letter to the editor.

Always sign your letter to the editor with your name and your company's name and address. You never know how much of your letter and "signature" they will print. Most newspapers and magazines accept letters by e-mail, making it easy to include your detailed e-mail signature. (See pages 151–52 for more on signatures.)

LETTER TO A COLUMNIST

When you write to a columnist, you can follow the same guidelines as when writing to the editor. However, when you write to the editor you can cover any topic in the whole publication. When writing to the columnist you are restricted to the focus of that column. The advantage of writing to a columnist is that they probably get fewer letters.

You might write to a columnist with a question, to tell a short story, or to provide some facts. Use the same approach you would in writing to the editor.

YOUR OWN ARTICLES

If you can have a conversation and write a letter, you can write an article. The secret is to just write. Most writing is imperfect the first time. Mine sure is. Edit and clean up later. The computer brings writing within everyone's reach. It is a giant leap forward from writing by hand or type-writer.

> Writing is easy. All you do is sit down
> at the typewriter and open a vein.
> — RED SMITH, PULITZER PRIZE–WINNER AND SPORTS COLUMNIST

Even if you don't think you are a good writer, you can easily turn out a competently written and interesting article. Here are a few pointers.

Write a tips list

This is an easy way to write an article. Just make a list of tips, and then dress it up. Most publications love these lists; they're easy to read and provide value for the readers. Try any or all of these:

- 10 reasons
- 9 reminders
- 8 secrets from the pros
- 7 habits
- 6 common questions
- 5 cost savers
- 4 cornerstones
- 3 key lessons
- 2 gems
- 1 gold nugget

Tell a story

Write about something that happened to you or someone you know. Personal stories of discovery work well. When you edit the story, take out the unnecessary details. Just make the point — don't punish readers with all the gritty details.

Write about things that annoy you

Just let it out. The passion you feel will fuel your thoughts. Don't worry about the form, grammar, and language as you write. But clean it all up later! It is a good idea to let someone else edit this brand of writing. They will not be as emotional as you are, and they will see things more clearly. You might write an article about "voice mail pet peeves" or "customer service that revolts you."

Expose myths and realities

State some common myths, then proceed to debunk them based on your expertise. This is where you can use unusual facts and figures.

Target your audience

For maximum effect, try to place your articles in publications that your market reads. But don't walk away from free publicity in other publications. Remember, everybody has alternative interests and they have friends and family who can spread the word. I was once surprised to get comments from a dentist about my article in a national sales magazine. You never know what your market reads.

Don't let numbers fool you. I had an article published in a big-city Saturday paper. It had a distribution of 1.5 million, yet I only received a few comments. But when I published in a national sales magazine with a distribution of 30,000, I got several calls and at least a dozen comments. Included were two requests to reprint that article in other publications.

> For every person who comments on your article, 100 people thought about it.

Remember:
- Not everybody reads.
- Not everybody looks at the name.
- If your picture is there, readers will see it before they see your name.
- Even if they read and like your article, few people will formally acknowledge it.
- Others will have digested your name for reference as an expert.

- In general, your name must be seen seven times to be remembered.
- People skim publications for familiar faces and names. Make your articles "skim catchers."

USE YOUR NAME, PHOTO, AND BIO

A colleague called me to say she had just read one of my articles and enjoyed it. This article did not carry my picture. She explained that she was reading it, then part way through, remarked to herself, "This sounds just like George Torok." To her surprise, when she glanced down to see who the author was — there was my name.

— *GEORGE*

YOUR OWN NEWSLETTER

You may guarantee print exposure by selling subscriptions to or giving away your own newsletter.

What you might include in your newsletter:

- Stories and photos from clients. The clients you feature will love it and request extra copies — be generous and give them lots.
- Tips you have compiled yourself or learned from other experts. Always give credit.
- "Q & A with the expert" (You!)
- Announcements of new services or products
- Information on related services
- A list of your favourite business-related books
- Seasonal reminders to your clients
- Trends in your industry
- Your editorial
- Letters from your clients
- Inspirational and humorous quotations

You might publish the newsletter by yourself or with a group of colleagues. I know of a few groups of consultants who pool their articles for a joint newsletter. Each writes about their specialty. Together, they

Newsie the customs

have a meatier newsletter. They increase their reach into the clients of their colleagues and they share the expense.

Consider gathering a group of related professionals to create a newsletter. Here are some possible combinations:

- Topic: *estate planning*
  lawyer, financial planner, banker, insurance specialist, funeral director
- Topic: *health care*
  doctor, dentist, pharmacist, chiropractor, psychiatrist
- Topic: *home maintenance*
  plumber, TV repair person, gardener, cleaning expert, electrician, deck builder, painter, window cleaner
- Topic: *home furnishing*
  carpets and flooring expert, furniture retailer, cabinet maker, bath accessory retailer, paint and wallpaper expert, appliance retailer
- Topic: *business services*
  computer sales and service professionals, telephone company representative, temporary help agent, accountant, security expert, training professional, printer, janitorial services expert, courier company representative

Here are some extra tips: Even if you give away your newsletter, print a price on it to show the value (not your cost). Do not date the issues; that way, you will get longer-term use out of each one. Instead, indicate the "issue number."

3.3 RADIO

I am sending messages across the ocean without a cable.
— *GUGLIELMO MARCONI TO AN INCREDULOUS AUDIENCE*

PUBLIC SERVICE ANNOUNCEMENTS

All radio stations are required by law to make free public service announcements, or PSAs. Unfortunately, they are usually run at non-peak listening periods. PSAs are not meant to provide companies with free advertising. But you might use them to announce events that you sponsor and that are open to the community — a contest, picnic, charity fundraiser, information seminar, or association event.

HOW TO GET ON RADIO TALK SHOWS

Identify the stations that have talk radio, especially those with programs that feature interviews with guests. Find themes that are a good fit for your message. Contact the program director — sometimes this could be the host. Explain your topic — it must be of value to the show's listeners. It is better to talk to the program director on the phone, since they want to hear how you sound. A boring expert is not welcome. They sound — well, boring. And on radio all you have is sound.

The show may or may not take you right away. Once you have made contact and established the possibility of interest, add them to your database of contacts and be persistent. Follow up by sending information and calling.

If you strike out with one show, try the others at the same station. The hosts often have a friendly (and sometimes not-so-friendly) competition between them. It helps if you have heard the show before you call; that way you can comment about a previous guest.

HOW TO PREPARE FOR THE RADIO INTERVIEW

So you've scheduled an interview — now you need to prepare. Ask for the details of when and where it will take place and how long it will last. There are three ways to conduct a radio interview: in person at the studio; over the phone; or in person with a tape recorder. If you have a choice, go to the studio. It is more exciting, and if you're excited, you'll sound more interesting. You will also meet the host, who might get to know you and like you. And it is easier to take part in a face-to-face interview.

Ask some questions. Will there be questions from callers? Ask about the host's usual approach. Will they support or challenge you? It helps if you have heard them and know their style. Are they caustic, are they crusading, are they the type to interrupt, and are they out to embarrass you? Most are not — but you don't want to get caught by surprise.

Arrive at the studio early. Wear comfortable clothes. On radio everyone looks good.

If you're doing the interview by phone, remove all possible distractions. Turn off the other phone lines, intercom, cell phone, and beeper. Close the window to muffle outside noises. Close your office door and post a "do not disturb" sign. Clear a space on your desk for your notes. Sit tall in a comfortable chair, or better yet, stand. By standing you sound clearer and may even think more clearly. If you have a headset for your phone, use it. Speaker phones do not sound clear enough, so don't use one. Keep a glass of water handy, but don't slurp on the air.

Decide on the one important message you want to deliver. Rehearse it a few times so it will sound powerful, natural, and memorable. Then look for the opportunity to work it in.

Keep a few notes in front of you. They should include the name of the host, the name of the program, and the call letters of the station. Try to use them once or twice in your interview. For example: "I am delighted to join you on *CFMU* today"; or "*George*, I imagine that the listeners of *Business in Motion* would like to hear the most important lesson I have learned."

The host will love you for plugging their show. They are more likely to support you during the interview and invite you back.

Your notes might also include a few points you want to mention, and any pertinent details you might be asked or want to give out, such as the date of an event, a phone number, or a web address.

Visit the washroom before you go on the air. That's one less thing to worry about.

PREPARING YOUR VOICE

Drink two or three glasses of lukewarm water before the interview. The water lubricates your throat. Breathe deeply, pushing your tummy out when you breathe in. This fills the lungs. Open the throat and relax the vocal chords by yawning. Warm up the vocal chords by humming. The slower you talk and the deeper your voice, the more believable and powerful you will sound. Avoid dairy products before the interview: milk and cheese will cause phlegm in your throat. Coffee and tea are also not good for your voice.

If you have a boring manner or difficult accent, visit a voice coach. You can find one by asking the local radio station or theatre groups for referrals.

HOW TO TALK ON THE AIR

Ask the host for instructions. Generally speaking, you want to be about six inches from the microphone. Talk to the mike, not to the host. Smile — it is noticeable in your voice. If you have notes, don't rustle paper; the mike will pick it up.

Most people talk too quietly on the air. You'll probably have to talk a little bit more slowly and loudly than you normally would. In this medium, your only tool for showing emotion is your voice, so use it. Answer questions calmly. Beware of cutting off the interviewer or answering too quickly, two habits that tend to make you sound nervous or defensive.

Don't refer to a private conversation you had with the interviewer off the air. This makes the listeners feel left out. Do not tell jokes. But do build in entertainment with humour, colourful analogies, and rhetorical questions.

Talk so the audience understands you and relates to you. Avoid jargon. If you must use technical language, explain it in layman's terms.

Watch your language. It may be okay to use coarse language in context (e.g., you can usually get away with saying "This customer was so frustrated, he was mad as hell" or "I would never damn the competition, but some of their clients do"), but remember you are not George Carlin or Howard Stern — nor do you want to be compared to them.

DEALING WITH THE UNEXPECTED QUESTION

What do you do when the host hits you with a totally unexpected question? The worst thing to do on radio is to leave "dead air." The next worst thing is to say "uhhhhhhhhhhhh." You must think while talking and sounding positive. Here are some responses that may buy you time to think:

"Wow, that is an incredible question, let me think that through."

"You know, that is a question I did not expect, but let me attempt to answer it."

"I am not surprised that you asked that, since it is a common misperception. The question that gets to the core of the issue is (state the question you want to answer)."

"Let me see if I understand the question (restate the question the way you want it to be phrased)."

"That brings to mind the time that (tell a short story that relates)."

If the question is unclear, ask your host to rephrase it, or answer the question you want to answer.

If you are given a multi-part question, you might say, "There are three parts to that question; let me answer the first part . . ." Then, "The second question was . . ." If you forget the question partway through, ask, "Did I answer your question?"

FINAL THOUGHTS ON SPEAKING ON THE RADIO

It is not a natural act to speak to a microphone, so don't be surprised if you feel awkard. With practice and by reviewing the tape after each interview, you should get better. It is more important that you get your message across than it is to use the precise words you planned before the interview. Sometimes spontaneous mistakes and malapropisms end up being your most quoted and memorable words.

MALAPROPISMS

Let's get that in black and writing.

Remember, there is only one taxpayer — you and me.

I don't want any information, I just want the facts.

If this thing starts to snowball it will catch fire right across the country.

We'd be giving them carte la blanche.

It's the most unheard-of thing I've ever heard of.

If somebody's gonna stab me in the back, I wanna be there.

Source: John Robert Colombo's New Canadian Quotations

How to Get Asked Back

Be a delightful, entertaining, and informative guest. Send a thank-you note to the host. Mention that you would love to be back. Send them your newsletter and/or brochure. Offer a repeat of the same topic and suggest a different slant. Follow up with them by mail, e-mail, and phone. Keep your media contacts on your database and keep them informed.

Get a Tape of the Interview

Bring your own cassette tape to the studio. Make sure you tell the host you are going to bring one to tape the show, and remind them of your intentions when you arrive.

After the interview, listen to the tape to see if you successfully conveyed your message. Did you sound clear and convincing? Did you just think of a better answer now? Don't worry, that's normal. Don't beat yourself up. Think instead about how you will do better next time. If the host has time, ask if they can suggest anything you could do differently next time. Almost nobody asks them to do this, so they will probably appreciate the question and may offer good advice.

Public and Community Radio

Most radio stations are commercial, but some are government-funded, such as the CBC in Canada and NPR in the United States. By their nature, public stations tend to have many talk shows and guests. Then there is community radio, which is usually operated by colleges and universities. They are non-profit and their mandate is to serve the community. As a result, they have many unique programs not heard on commercial radio. They are supported by listener donations and subsidies and use minimal, if any, advertising. Typically, community radio stations do not have big audiences, but they are targeted groups. It may be easier to get an interview on community radio, especially if your message serves the community's interests.

Your Own Program or Series

You might feel so bold as to host your very own radio show, either on commercial or community radio. Naturally, it is far easier to get a show on community radio stations, which are always looking for local content.

Try contacting the radio station's program director with your idea. You can choose from several formats:

- you could conduct interviews with guests, in spots that could vary from five minutes to one hour
- you could host a phone-in show, where you are the expert (à la Dr. Laura)
- you could deliver a 30-second or two-minute tip of the day

BUSINESS IN MOTION

For many years I have hosted the weekly radio show called *Business in Motion* on 93.3 CFMU at McMaster University in Hamilton, Ontario. I interview outstanding business guests from different industries. They talk about the changes they have made, the obstacles they have faced, and how they grow. Being the host of the radio show enhances my credibility with the clients who hire me for speaking. My biography and introduction mention my radio show. When I speak I often mention lessons from my radio show. It positions me as "the speaker with the radio show." And because I interview CEOs of well-known companies, it enhances my image as a business expert.

— *GEORGE*

3.4 TELEVISION

The medium is the message.
— *MARSHALL MCLUHAN*

HOW TO GET ON TELEVISION

To get yourself on TV, you'll want to follow the same procedures you would use for getting on radio. The extra challenge when it comes to TV is that if you're on camera, you need to sound good *and* look interesting.

But take heart: if you sound good but don't look so great, the producers can always move the camera to the show's host or show pictures of something related to your talk.

NATIONAL, LOCAL, COMMUNITY, AND SPECIALTY CHANNELS
TV stations come in four varieties.

1. The *national networks* are the hardest to get on but the most glamorous. To be invited to appear on a national network, you must have a topic that will appeal to groups across the country and you must appear to be a national expert.
2. If you are active locally, it is fairly simple to get on the *local station* for a two- or five-minute spot.
3. *Community cable channels* are most open to local guests. As with community radio, they have a requirement to feature local issues and personalities. Not only can you get short interview spots, but you might easily get frequent appearances. You could even have your own show, but don't expect to get paid — community TV and radio stations are mostly run by volunteers. Consider the work an opportunity for local exposure and practice for when you hit the national networks.
4. *Specialty channels* need content. If you are an expert in a topic related to one of these specialties, their doors are likely to be open to you.

> I didn't know it then, but one of the secrets of success on television is, if you can't be beautiful, be memorable.
> — BRIAN LINEHAN, *TV HOST*

PREPARING FOR TV
The show will most likely be filmed in the studio, although they might be shooting "on location." When it comes to preparing your voice, do everything you would do if you were on radio. For TV you must be conscious of how you look. Dress appropriately for the image you wish to convey. If you are talking about rock climbing you should dress in rock-climbing garb. If you are representing your business, look the part. Viewers will judge what you say based on how you look. Keep in mind also that viewers who are surfing the channels may tune in if you look interesting.

Loosen up before you go on, so you can sit or stand tall while looking comfortable. Check yourself in the mirror just before you go. Smile and wink at yourself in the mirror to help relax and look friendly.

> And now the sequence of events in no particular order.
> — DAN RATHER, *TV NEWS ANCHOR*

HOW TO TALK ON THE AIR

All the guidelines for talking on the radio apply here, but there are a few more. Ask the host for directions: where should you stand, sit, look? You will probably be given a lapel mike; if you are, remember not to turn your head too far, or the mike will not pick up your words of wisdom. But show expression in your face. If you are in the studio you must limit your hand motions. They will only distract. Be careful of nervous eye movement. The audience will label you as shifty and untrustworthy.

Dress simply. Don't wear distracting accessories, such as outlandish ties or dangling earrings. Don't fidget. *Remember to smile.*

> Do you mind if I sit back a little? Because your breath is very bad.
> — DONALD TRUMP, *TO TALK-SHOW HOST LARRY KING IN 1989*

3.5 THE INTERNET

> Radio has no future.
> X-rays are clearly a hoax.
> The aeroplane is scientifically impossible.
> — ROYAL SOCIETY PRESIDENT LORD KELVIN, *1897–99*

> The atom bomb will never go off
> — and I speak as an expert in explosives.
> — U.S. ADMIRAL WILLIAM LEAHY IN *1945*

> Television won't matter in your lifetime or mine.
> — RADIO TIMES *EDITOR REX LAMBERT, 1936*

> Everything that can be invented has been invented.
> — *DIRECTOR OF THE U.S. PATENT OFFICE, 1899*

Everyone can make a mistake. Even Bill Gates missed hopping on the Internet in the early days. But Bill learned fast and put the Internet to work; he set a new course for Microsoft and quickly came to dominate his industry.

The important lesson is that he realized that business must be on the Internet to grow and survive. If you have not yet started to harness the power of the Internet you might be forgiven. But you had better learn fast.

> The Internet will have the biggest impact on business
> since the invention of the personal computer.
> The impact of the Internet on marketing will equal that
> of the creation of the printing press.

Because the Internet and the World Wide Web are changing so rapidly, almost anything written about it here will be out of date when this book goes to print. Consequently, these tips are general in nature. The best place to learn about the Internet is on the Internet. Sign on and surf. But don't do it during prime business hours when you should be making calls and serving clients.

RESEARCH

Do your market research on the Internet. You can find government statistics, economic indicators, and financial reports. Good places to start looking for business information are the web sites of business magazines, government small-business help centres, and banks. Use your browser and search engines to check out your competition, your clients, and your suppliers. Subscribe to e-mail newsletters to keep up on topics important to your business. Through e-mail, forums, and chat rooms, you can have a network of advisers and colleagues all around the world.

YOUR WEB PAGE

How is a web page different from a web site? Think of a web site as a book or magazine. The whole book/site might contain material from only one author/owner. That one owner has control and responsibility for the site — all the maintenance, promotion, and costs. The owner can also choose a unique domain name (more about domain names later).

The web-site owner can invite others to use "pages" on the site and charge a kind of "page rental" fee to cover some of the maintenance costs. With enough renters, owning a web site could be a profitable business in itself. At the same time, page renters do not have the full cost or commitment involved in having their own web sites.

Having a web page on someone else's web site is a good place to start out in establishing your Internet presence. Should you eventually decide to get your own web site, don't automatically cancel any rented web pages you may have, especially if they form part of a site that is relevant to your business. Just make sure you keep track of where you appear. You should also ask related web sites to include a link to your own.

ADVANTAGES

If you are on the web, you can direct folks to your page and proudly answer "Yes" to that proverbial question, "Are you on the web?"

You can post information about your company.

It will cost less than your own site.

It is a good place to start to learn about web sites.

DISADVANTAGES

You will not have a distinctive web address. It will be a subsection of someone else's site.

You may have to follow the guidelines of the site owner.

You may not want to be associated with some of the other page owners on that site.

HOW TO GET A WEB PAGE

Your ISP (Internet Service Provider) may offer the service.

Your association might offer pages for members on its site.

You might form a group with one or more colleagues — just like a group newsletter.

You might join a services listing; these are sometimes called sales malls.

YOUR WEB SITE

Once you have a web site, you have arrived in cyberspace. Then you own real estate in this new frontier. In cyberspace some rules of real estate are different. There is unlimited supply, so owning real estate does not guarantee anything. Location is not important, but address and ease of discovery are crucial.

> Check our web sites at www.PeterUrsBender.com
> and www.Torok.com

Some lessons from real estate do apply. Undeveloped and badly planned real estate is worthless. It is best to define your purpose before you start building. Your site must look good and provide value. You should continue to improve and renovate your site.

First decide what you want your site to do and whom you want to attract. Design the site to fit the purpose. Hopefully your purpose is more than just to "get on the web" — a web site is a business tool, not an end in itself.

Your purpose might be:

web-site must have

- to list a catalogue of your products and services
- to be a reference site with tons of information for your clients
- to find new clients
- to provide a convenient place for media and clients to download your published works
- to take online orders for products
- to offer a showcase for new ideas and developments in your industry.

Your site should reflect your image, just as your stationery should. So get it done professionally. If you are a professional web-site designer, do it yourself. But if you are not, hire someone to do a good job. If you want something simple, it does not have to be expensive. I have discovered some good sites developed by students who have reasonable rates.

Make sure to keep your business site separate from your personal or family site.

How to Get Others to Visit Your Site

Announce your web site when it is launched. Also announce major renovations. Send those announcements via e-mail and to the regular media by news release.

Send announcements to the online news magazines.

Send a news release when your site receives awards or reaches milestones, such as the one-year anniversary or the one millionth visit, or when it is named the "hot site of the day."

Put your web site and e-mail on all your printed material — cards, letterhead, invoices, and flyers.

Send your web address and short synopsis to business publications that list interesting web sites. Include both paper publications and online publications.

Snail mail post cards to clients, prospects, and media. Have these post cards printed with an image of your home page, with your URL (web address) prominently displayed.

Include your URL in your e-mail signature along with a reason to visit.

Register your web site with the major search engines and directories.

Announce your web site address on your voice mail greeting.

Links

Build links to other sites that relate and complement your site. Ask those sites for reciprocal links to yours. You should be able to have your association link to your site, especially if they have a member listing.

What You Might Have on Your Site

You can offer all the choices you might in your own newsletter. Consider including:

Cnoved for web site

- descriptions of your products and services
- your articles
- your news releases
- links to your associates
- detailed information behind a door that only "members" or privileged clients can access
- "ask the expert" (you) bulletin board
- product ordering
- list of key clients (also known as a "brag list")
- customer testimonials
- your credentials
- your photo
- company mission and slogan
- your pricing structure, if it is appropriate for your business and positioning
- and a lot more possibilities . . .

E-MAIL

Check your e-mail daily and respond to incoming messages quickly. We expect you to. Sending e-mail should be like having one-to-one conversations. It can help you with relationship building. Be friendly and personal in your writing style, and make your messages short and concise. It shows that you respect others and yourself.

Because e-mail is easy and fast, too many adopt a casual attitude to their language and grammar. Readers can only judge you by what they see. Messages full of typos do not feel like quality.

Remember that e-mail is print. Don't print anything you don't want repeated or read by anyone. Even private e-mail can be intercepted, misrouted, copied, or forwarded in error or with malice.

Never, never, never write e-mail in anger. At the least, it can be very embarrassing; at worst, it could land you in court. It is so easy to make this mistake because e-mail is sent instantaneously. We write and send without proofreading or thinking. If there is any chance your e-mail might be misunderstood, save it for a day and then edit it.

E-mail signatures

AUTO RESPONDER

This is a service that will send an automatic reply to e-mail sent to a certain address (e.g., info@torok.com). It works somewhat like fax on demand, and saves time when you get a lot of standard questions. Talk to your ISP to set these up.

E-MAIL SIGNATURE

Most e-mail software allows you to have what is called a "signature," or standard message, automatically appended to the bottom of your outgoing e-mail. Some e-mail software further allows you to create and pick from more than one signature. For example, you might have a short signature for personal messages and a long one that includes a special message for business purposes. Think of your signatures as your personal sandwich-board signs. For ideas on what to include in your signature, look at what other people are doing. You might wish to include some of the following:

- your name
- company name
- mailing address
- phone and fax numbers
- web-site address along with invitation to visit the site
- slogan
- short description of what you sell
- a free offer (use this to attract others to your web site or sign up for your newsletter)
- announcement of a special event

It is polite to turn your signature off for personal e-mail messages. No need to beat your friends over the head with your advertising messages. Also turn it off for very short messages — it looks funny if your signature is longer than your message.

Peter Urs Bender, CSP
Author of "Secrets of Power Presentations"
(a Canadian bestseller, with over 100,000 copies in print;
now also translated into French, German, Indonesian, and Russian)
and "Leadership from Within" (published by Stoddart, Canada)

108–150 Palmdale Drive, Toronto, ON, Canada, M1T 3M7
Phone (416) 491-6690 Fax: (416) 490-0375
To order the audio cassette album or softcover copy of
the books, call Books for Business: 1-800-668-9372

Visit:
www.PeterUrsBender.com
www.Torok.com

This is my long signature, so I use it only for business messages. For personal messages, I might use the following:

Peter Urs Bender
(416) 491-6690

Life is either a daring adventure or nothing.
Helen Keller

DOMAIN NAME

In the long signature above, the web sites listed have the domain names "PeterUrsBender.com" and "Torok.com." Essentially, the domain is the address you type in to get directly to the web site. It is better to have a short, direct domain name than it is to have one like "PeterUrsBender. ISPprovider.com" or "Internetcompany.com/Gtorok." The former shows a subdomain of the domain "ISPprovider.com." The latter represents the format for a web page on the domain "Internetcompany.com."

The easier the domain name is to remember, the easier it is for prospects to visit. And once you've registered your name, no one else can use it. For more information on domain names and how to register, please go to www.PowerMarketing.ca.

Pick a simple domain name, so all prospects need do is remember that name and type it in — no phone numbers, street addresses, or codes. If you need to change your ISP, you can take your domain name with you. No need to reprint all your stationery.

Here's another advantage: Having a domain name makes you look bigger than you are. You can look as big as Microsoft.com or IBM.com.

YOUR ONLINE NEWSLETTER

This is the greatest way to publish a newsletter. Distribution is virtually free. You write the newsletter, then send it to the people on your list, who can forward it on to their own contacts if they like.

Your online newsletter may contain everything that you would use in a paper newsletter. I recommend you keep it short. Of the several newsletters I receive, some are several pages long, and some are quick tips with just a few lines. I prefer the quick tips because I have time to read them.

When you start your newsletter you can create the distribution list in your e-mail program under a nickname. When you send your newsletter to the nickname, it is automatically sent to everyone on that list. Address the nickname as a blind carbon copy (BCC). That way each receiver is not forced to read through a long list of e-mail addresses before they get to the meat of your message. Besides, it is bad manners to distribute other people's e-mail addresses without permission.

Always include short instructions to the receiver on how to stop receiving the newsletter. And honour those requests.

Never send a newsletter to someone who has not requested it. Encourage readers to sign up for your newsletter through your web site, or via personal e-mail.

LISTSERV

When your list gets big and keeps growing, get a listserv (also called a list server or list manager). This type of software allows you to automate the distribution of your newsletter and the addition and deletion of names. Treat your list of e-mail addresses with respect. You might share it with another business to do a joint promotion. But do not abuse your readers with junk or "spam."

"Spam" is junk e-mail that is sent to hundreds and often thousands of addresses. It is usually blatant advertising. The sender, if well-intentioned, is playing the numbers game: send out tons of garbage and some will buy. At worst it just costs time and clutters up the information highway.

FORUMS

Take part in discussion forums to learn more about a topic. Offer to lead a discussion forum on your area of expertise. You might appear as a guest discussion leader or even sponsor your own forum. If you do, plan to make regular appearances. Citizens of cyberspace are very impatient.

GETTING PUBLISHED ONLINE

Everything that you publish on paper can be published online. In fact, it is even easier to be published online and there may be more venues. Submit your ideas to online news magazines that publish articles on their site, just like a regular magazine. If they publish your article, get them to include hot links to your e-mail and web site next to your name and/or photo.

Many paper publications publish some of their content on their web sites. You might find one of your articles from a print publication at their web site. Ask them for hot links.

Try hooking up with other businesses that have free or paid online newsletters. They are always looking for words of value to their subscribers.

Every time you publish online, regardless of the venue, try to give readers a reason for visiting your web site. You might offer a free subscription to your online newsletter or a free tips list.

INTERNET NOTES

The number one Internet language is English. Number two is Spanish.

Internet service provider America OnLine (AOL) has more subscribers than the ten largest newspapers in the United States.

The Internet is a product of the cold war.

TRADITIONAL MEDIA ONLINE

Most newspapers, magazines, radio stations, and television networks have their own web sites. You can use the Internet to find, contact, and research these organizations. You can send news releases online; and some sites even allow you to mass distribute your news release. It is a sure sign of the power of the Internet that all the traditional media are online. They have some of the best sites. And well they should — they already know about reaching mass audiences.

INTERNET RADIO

Hot on the heels of online newsletters and magazines are Internet radio and Internet TV. These new developments will open up more media marketing channels for you. For technical reasons, audio is easier to transmit than video. On Internet radio, which is already up and working at many sites, you can be interviewed just like on regular radio. And you can send others to the site to click on the interview anytime and play it. As this new medium grows, there will be an increased need for guests and hosts. Give it a shot.

It will be very tough to keep up with all this technology. But working with all forms of the media can be fun and rewarding for your business. As they say in show business, *break a leg*.

SUMMARY
SECRETS OF MEDIA

- If you must pay for publicity, don't advertise. Sponsor.
- Cultivate relationships with your media contacts. Stay in touch. Thank them for any exposure and send them sweets.
- Send news releases regularly. Make them skim catchers.
- Write articles that offer value to readers and make sure your name, number, and photo are printed. Write to the editor, a columnist, or a reporter.
- Use your web site and e-mail as marketing tools. Make your e-mail signature a miniature signboard and offer e-mail newsletters.

Spend $1 and you will get 80 cents in value.

But if you want 100 times your return —

be creative and tap into your intangible resources.

— George Torok

Leverage

If I had a lever long enough
I could move the world.
— *Archimedes*

STRATEGY
FOUR

If I said, "I bet you $20 that I can lift a car with my own strength," you might take one look at me (I'm no Arnold Schwarzenegger) and take that bet. Then I would take your money as I set up the jack and lifted the car.

"Wait a minute," you'd stammer, "You said you'd lift it with your own strength — that's no fair." And I'd point out, "The jack is not lifting the car. It is the tool that I use to lever my strength. The jack does not make me stronger but it helps me focus my limited strength to do the job. With the lever I am lifting the car by using my strength in a smarter way."

In your business you have limited resources, but if you focus those resources you can leverage your strength to compete with big business. Power Marketing is like the jack. It helps you create amazing feats of marketing.

In this chapter we will examine the resources you have at your disposal and the three key principles you can use to leverage those resources into something greater. You'll also learn about several Power Marketing tools you can use to make your work easier.

RESOURCES TO BE LEVERAGED

You already have what it takes to start leveraging. Some of the limited resources you can expand and grow include:

Intangibles

- time
- confidence
- credibility
- skills
- strengths
- knowledge

Tangibles

- money
- customers
- staff
- quality level
- equipment
- technology
- information

Each of these resources will be limited for different reasons, and most limits are temporary. The exception is time. Time is the most important resource you have, precisely because it is limited. You only have twenty-four hours in your day — you can't change that. But at least on this dimension, you are equal to everyone else. And if you use your time more effectively you get more ROT (return on time). You may have learned about the importance of ROI (return on investment), but it's just as crucial to improve your ROT. Later in this chapter we will explore concrete ways to do this (see the section "Time and Luck").

The rest of the intangibles are resources over which you have direct control. *After time, confidence is the next most valuable resource you have.* You can't get it from anywhere or anyone. It is within you. You can only allow yourself to let it out. I believe that confidence is the single most important personal quality to possess if you're going to succeed.

Even if you only have small quantities of the tangibles, such as money, you can begin working to gain more. You have only indirect control over the tangibles, but it's crucial to remember that the methods you use to deploy your intangibles will affect your tangibles. For example, how you use your time, skills, and credibility will determine the number of customers you have. How you use your people skills will affect the value of your staff.

The tangibles may look more valuable because they are measurable. Use them to maximize their marketing impact. But if your competition has greater quantities of tangible resources than you do, you can still compete and win. You can focus on leveraging your abundant supply of intangibles. The intangibles of time, confidence, and skills will beat money if properly implemented. That is why, as they say, "a fool and his money are soon parted." If you use both intangibles and tangibles, and intelligently make them work together, that is real Power Marketing.

You can have a small amount of money and still compete with the big guys. The secret is to avoid going head-to-head with someone bigger and stronger than you. Instead, pick your angle and a lever. David did not try to wrestle Goliath; he chose instead to slay the giant with an unimposing slingshot. If you are in small business, think like a David.

> Great works are performed not by strength,
> but by perseverance.
> — SAMUEL JOHNSON

PRINCIPLES AND TOOLS

Let's take a closer look at the basic principles and tools of leveraging. The principles are the fundamental approaches you take to achieving leverage. The tools are the specific tips and techniques used to implement those principles.

Three Principles of Leverage	*Some Tools*
1. Focus	Books
2. Be Unique	Tapes
3. Be Creative	Presentations
	Strengths/Weaknesses
	Obstacles
	The 3Rs
	Negotiation

important

As you can see, the principles are not unrelated — for example, it often takes real creativity to be unique. And when you do something unique, you are *focusing* your talents in a special way. So often you will be implementing two or three principles at once.

In the same way, all of the tools you see listed can help you apply any one of these principles — and leverage your limited resources into powerful marketing strategies.

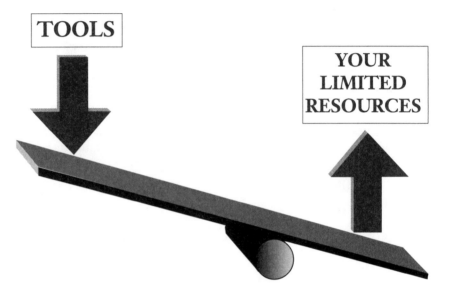

Let's apply the car-and-jack analogy to the above diagram. The principle used in this case is "focus" — that is your lever. The limited resource is your strength — if you were strong enough you could lift the car without the jack. The tool used is the technology of the jack. It is simple technology, but it's all that's needed for this particular task. The result is that your limited resource — strength — accomplishes a bigger feat than imagined. You lifted a car!

Use leverage to get more out of your time, money, and experience. It will boost your credibility, exposure, and self-confidence. If you do not use leverage, your resources will tend to appear just as they are or even less than they are — maybe flat and unimpressive. In today's competitive world, everything is relative and you are being compared with the competition.

But when you use the right tools to leverage your resources, the same resources will appear stronger and bigger, and they'll have greater impact.

> Do what you can, with what you have, where you are.
> — THEODORE ROOSEVELT

4.1 FOCUS

> To focus you must point at one thing.

You've already seen how you can lift a car with your own strength. The jack does not make you stronger — it simply allows you to focus. This is such a simple concept that it can be easily overlooked.

A diamond cutter cuts the world's hardest substance by focusing the chisel on the flaw. If he misses his target, the diamond shatters and a valuable gem becomes industrial sandpaper. Similarly, the karate student learns to focus her punch to break a brick.

Focus yourself in an area where you want to be known. You cannot be master of everything. I started by focusing on "presentation skills," or how to present in front of a group.

— PETER

> If there is no wind, row.
> — LATIN PROVERB

Focus is necessary to get what you want. If you are job hunting and your attitude is that any job will do, it increases the likelihood that you will not get any job. When a human resources manager asks you what job you are applying for, and you say that you will take *anything*, you're sending the message that you can't *do* anything.

Yet some people find it very difficult to focus. Why is this so? It's not because it takes more energy to focus. A laser uses less energy than a broad, unfocused beam of light does. Yet the laser is more powerful. The reality is that in order to focus, you must do *less*. You must give up something else for the one thing you focus on. Why do some people surf television channels using the remote control device? Because they might miss something on the other channels. They are so afraid to miss something that they do not focus on one program. This may be okay for leisure time, but it can be a killer habit in business.

HOW CAN YOU FOCUS YOUR MARKETING EFFORTS?

First, start by focusing your business. What business are you in? You are not focused if you shampoo rugs, run a grocery store, consult on computer systems, sell crafts, and photograph weddings — all at the same time. This is not to say that you can't have more than one business, but if you do, remember to only concentrate on one at a time.

No one can say they don't know how to focus. We all focused when we learned to walk, talk, read, ride a bike, pass our driver's licences. And how did we do that? By intuitively following the guidelines listed below for proper focus:

1. Know, envision, and clearly state what you want.
2. Really want it. As an infant you wanted to learn to walk. You didn't let a few dozen or a hundred falls stop you. You focused and pressed on.
3. Prioritize. If you could do only one thing, what would it be? What would be next? When you write your news releases to the media, you put your most important message first because the reader may never get past that first line. In other words, you focus your message.
4. Know what you are willing to give up to get what you want. If you want to learn another language, you have to give up time you might have spent in leisure in order to study. To run your own business, you give up the security of a regular paycheque.
5. Practise saying no. Acknowledge your limited resources, especially your time, and be firm in declining social engagements, requests for volunteer help, or even new contracts in order to focus on the work you really need to do. And if you do good work, most people will respect you for saying no when you have to.
6. Know how to say no to yourself. When you are offered opportunities outside your area of expertise, you may wish to take them on simply because they are

interesting. But you must remind yourself what you want to be known for and stick to it.

7. Be willing to take short steps or make adjustments as long as you are moving in the right direction. If your goal is to get on national television, take any media interviews that get you exposure and move in the direction of your goal. You don't climb Mount Everest in a straight line. There are some detours, delays, and course corrections on the way to the peak.

Now let's focus your marketing efforts. Remember that you need this focus because you have limited resources. Make a marketing plan and keep it simple. Know what you want to do (choose some ideas from this book), how often you will do it, and how much time and money you will spend on it over the next six months.

For example, if you plan to join an association and be on the board, you might budget time and money for membership fees and the lunch fees for one general meeting and one board meeting per month. If you plan to send out one news release each month, you might allocate four hours and $100 per month. Create a plan you can realistically follow.

Check your progress. Record what you spend, stick to the plan, and review periodically. Make adjustments. Try not to make drastic changes, since some things take time to pay off. Marketing is a long-term commitment.

Created plan I can follow - stay on track.

4.2 BE UNIQUE

❚ Be unique, be noticed, be remembered.

While contemplating your focus you discovered that you must point. But point where? To determine your direction, it helps to consider a second principle for leveraging your resources: being unique.

Has anyone ever told you that you are "different"? If so, ask them, "In what way?" Ask them how that helps you or hurts you. Then capitalize on your uniqueness. This is the strongest way to build Brand *You*.

Are you the plumber that juggles? The lawyer who rides a motorcycle?

Capitalize on your uniqueness

Bender and Torok

The computer technician who wears a doctor's frock? If you don't yet feel unique, here are several techniques for finding and creating that perception of individuality.

POSITIONING

Stake out your ground and announce it to the world. Be number one in your market. If you can't be number one in an existing market, create a new category.

Coke was well entrenched as the old established product, having been in the marketplace for over 100 years. Pepsi took the opposite swing and called itself "the choice of a new generation." Then, depending on whom you believe, Coke got nervous and blinked by changing the formula. They tried to move from their position to Pepsi's. After the uproar they scrambled back to regain their original position with Coke Classic. Coke had a reputation and status in the minds of consumers. When they tried to change their image to win over the "young rebel" crowd, it was too much of a stretch. It ended up confusing rather than attracting customers.

Here are some examples of effective positioning:

7-Up could not compete in the cola wars so they billed themselves as the Uncola.

Hertz was number one in the rental car business so Avis adopted the slogan "we try harder."

When the big Canadian banks were talking merger, one of the banks bought National Trust, leaving Canada Trust as the largest remaining "independent" trust company. Canada Trust began to advertise itself as the alternative to the big banks.

> When everyone is fighting over the mountain top,
> stake out your territory in the valley, or on another peak.

HOW CAN YOU FIND YOUR NICHE?

Do this

1. *Examine the market.*
   Discover who is the best in your market.

Describe what they do best. Why are they so successful?

Define the demographics and major needs of the market.

Think about what changes technology will have on this market.

Look at methods of product delivery. How could they be changed?

Test your ideas on potential customers. Your friends are not a good measure of the market reaction.

2. *Examine yourself.**

Describe your successes. Why did you succeed?

How do your friends/bosses/staff describe you?

How do your clients describe you?

What do you do better than most people you know?

What do you do well but don't really like to do?

On what tasks do you usually fail or perform poorly?

Can you overcome your weaknesses by ignoring, correcting, or compensating for them? What do you do that makes you feel good?

What have you done that has delighted others?

* For more help on self-analysis and tips on bringing out your personal strengths, read *Leadership from Within*, by Peter Urs Bender (Stoddart, 1997).

CREATE YOUR OWN CATEGORY OR BRAND

It is better to be first in your market than to be better. Betamax, deemed by most to be the superior product, lost to VHS in the VCR war. Although many admit the Macintosh to be a better computer, they still go with the entrenched IBM-compatible.

The first company in any market has an amazing advantage, because trying to be better than an established product is a tougher battle to fight. It is easier and more profitable to be first — then you can focus on maintaining your lead.

Brands that were first in their market and still dominate

Brand	Product Type
Coke	cola
Heineken	beer imported into North America

The 1st inside out solution

Miller Light	U.S. domestic light beer
Harvard	U.S. colleges
Jeep	four-wheel-drive vehicles
Acura	Japanese luxury cars
Chrysler	minivans
Hewlett-Packard	desktop laser printer
Gillette	safety razor
Hayes	computer modem
Gatorade	sports drink
Thomas	English muffins
Roger Bannister	four-minute miler
Neil Armstrong	moonwalker
You	*(fill in the blank)*

There can be many "number ones" within larger categories. For example:

U.S. Presidents

Who was the first U.S. president?	George Washington
Who was the first Catholic president?	John F. Kennedy

Flight

Who made the first solo flight across the Atlantic?	Charles Lindbergh
Do you know who was the third?	(Amelia Earhart was the third person to solo across the Atlantic. Most don't know that. But we do know her as the *first woman* to solo across the Atlantic.)
Who made the first powered flight?	The Wright brothers
Who was the first to break the sound barrier?	Chuck Yeager
Who was the first ace fighter pilot?	The Red Baron

Being first isn't always enough to be remembered. Creative positioning and marketing can make a "second" appear to be a first.

Space Flight

Who was the first man in space?	Yuri Gagarin of the USSR
Who was the first American in space?	Alan Shepard
Who was the first American in orbit?	John Glenn

Many forget about Yuri Gagarin and Alan Shepard. But most remember that John Glenn was first at something to do with space. Did Glenn get better marketing? I think so.

In each of the above examples who was second? Who cares?

Do you believe there can only be one first within a category? Well then, consider mountain climbing. Let's be even more specific — climbing Mount Everest. Who was the first? Sir Edmund Hilary, of course. But can there be any more firsts for climbing Mount Everest? Yes.

First Canadian
First American
First German
First woman
First up the north face
First up the south face
First to ski down
First without an oxygen supply
First blind climber

Each of the above would be significant achievements, but we don't want to get carried away. For example, these would probably not be particularly notable:

First left-handed climber
First blonde
First bald guy
First . . . enough already!

Sometimes the first in the market drops the ball and loses their position. Xerox invented the photocopier and dominated the market until the early seventies. Then they got cocky and were caught napping by the Japanese. Today you are more likely to see a Canon, Sharp, Toshiba, Panasonic, or Mita than a Xerox photocopier. But people still say, "Could you Xerox some copies for me?"

Xerox was also the first with the personal computer, but they failed to capitalize on that discovery. Being first in your market gives you tremendous advantage but it does not make you invulnerable. Stay awake. When you are number one you will attract imitators. So when you take the lead, keep moving.

> The first person to beat the four-minute mile record,
> Roger Bannister, passed his competition, John Landy,
> as John was looking over his other shoulder for Roger.

4.3 BE CREATIVE

It sounds contradictory at first, but to be unique you don't necessarily have to be original. Madonna is unique but she has patterned herself after Marilyn Monroe. It is okay to borrow ideas and concepts from other companies, products, and industries. You can even take ideas from history, nature, and fantasy.

Your ideas don't have to be brand new. Look to other industries, then tweak their ideas to fit your business. Uncover old concepts and bring them back. A doctor that makes house calls would be unique today, but many years ago that was the norm.

Reuse and recycle your own ideas and material. If you are a consultant, write a tips sheet as a gift for customers. Make it a news release. Turn it into an article. Collect a bunch of articles to create a booklet. Turn the booklet into a speech, and the speech into a tape. You can give the tape away to customers, and announce your giveaway with a news release. And so on . . .

In 1896, Baron Pierre de Coubertin, a French educator, instituted the modern Olympic Games, modelled on the competition that began in Athens in 776 B.C. It rivals the United Nations for internationalism. The idea was over 1,000 years old! But it was still a good idea.

The Brothers Grimm first published the story of Snow White and the Seven Dwarfs in 1815. They did not originate the story — they merely collected folk tales. Disney debuted it as an animated movie in 1937, and continues to rework and reissue the film about every seven years.

Disney leverages a movie like *Aladdin* into videos, clothes, books, lunch boxes, theme parks, and other products. They keep finding ways to make money from the original idea. Look at how hard Mickey Mouse works for Disney, decades after Walt's original sketches.

When the city of Toronto was choosing a name for its new NBA team (which came to be called the Raptors), one of the important criteria was the "leverage factor." The name had to be one they could sell as dolls, mascots, T-shirts, crests, and other merchandise.

USING YOUR STRENGTHS CREATIVELY

You can't be all things to all people. Find out what you are really good at, and make it your trademark. It might be that you are fast, thorough, fun to deal with, convenient, cost competitive — whatever it is, take advantage of it. Understand the problem

Don't be shy to use your strengths. You might be gifted in computer matters, methodical, very attractive, well educated, or from a connected family. Everyone has strengths — use them.

USING YOUR WEAKNESSES CREATIVELY

You might be preoccupied with thoughts like "If only I had a Ph.D.," "If only I was taller, thinner, whatever." Forget the "if-onlys." Ignore them or use them.

Buckley's cough syrup successfully used the memorable and effective positioning statement, "It tastes bad but it works."

Bill Gates never completed college. That should be a negative. Instead it is viewed as proof that he was focused on his business vision.

OVERCOMING OBSTACLES

I am not a natural born speaker. In fact I had three strikes against me. One, I came to Canada at the age of twenty-three to learn English. I have been here over twenty-five years and some of my friends say that if I stay here another twenty-five years I might yet learn English. In other words, my English is less than perfect. Two, my background is accounting in a Swiss bank. Swiss bankers do not tend to be outgoing, dynamic speakers! Three, I have fought with dyslexia all my life. That made it extremely difficult for me to read, write, and learn. If I had applied for a job as a public speaker with these obstacles on my résumé — well, you know what they would have said. So I made my own way and today I am called "Canada's Presentation Guru" and I have published three books. I still speak with a Swiss accent — which I once felt was another disadvantage — but today it is just part of what makes me unique and memorable.
— *PETER*

WEAKNESS INTO STRENGTH

I met Nancy Miller at a National Speakers Association convention. She had real impact — not by what she said but by how she said it.

We talked in the crowded hallway between sessions. When she gave me her card I noticed the photograph. It was the image of a woman standing with one leg and one crutch. I examined the photo closer, then looked her up and down. It was Nancy in the picture. This was the first time I noticed her disability. It impressed me that she used that as her symbol.

In the speaking business, many people forget our names, but it is easy to ask for "the woman with one leg." Even more memorable was the message emblazoned on her card: "The Power of One."
— *GEORGE*

USING OBSTACLES AND DISASTERS CREATIVELY

As an entrepreneur you will run into many obstacles, but most turn out to be temporary. Whatever you think is holding you back today can usually be overcome tomorrow.

Ask yourself, "What's stopping me?"

Once you have answered that, ask, "Why?"

Keep asking why until you discover the root of the obstacle.

Then ask yourself, "What must I do to change this?"

FEAR INTO SUCCESS

I was terrified to speak in public. Yet I started teaching "Effective Persuasion," a sales course at Ryerson Polytechnic University in Toronto. I did not need the aggravation or the extra money at that time. I was doing well in sales. One-on-one I was very good — in front of a group I was jelly.

I wanted to overcome this fear. I found that in order to teach, I had to learn very fast. The more I taught, the more I learned, and the better I became. After twelve years of part-time teaching I decided to launch my own speaking business. Many thought I was foolish to give up both my sales job and the part-time teaching. But I knew that I had to focus on where I wanted to go. I succeeded because I didn't allow myself any other options.

— *PETER*

❙ A plane climbs faster into the wind.

Ray Charles was six years old when glaucoma robbed him of his sight, but he had a dream of becoming a musician. How did he triumph? "The power of visualization," says Charles. "Regardless of how bad things got on the outside, I kept a clear picture in my head. I saw myself as a recording star."

If you are thinking, "Yeah, but . . . ," consider this list of successful people who never finished grade school:

Andrew Carnegie	American industrialist and philanthropist
Charlie Chaplin	British actor and film director
Charles Dickens	British novelist

Thomas Edison	American inventor
Claude Monet	French painter
John Philip Sousa	American bandleader and composer
Mark Twain	American humourist and writer

You are a composite of where you have been and what you have done, but your past does not determine what you might do or become. Everyone starts somewhere; often you must do some other job until you find the right career for you. Many successful people have had some unlikely "prior careers."

Personality	*Former Job*
Johnny Carson, talk show host	magician
Sean Connery, actor	bricklayer and truck driver
Gerald Ford, former U.S. president	male model
Albert Einstein, physicist	patent office clerk
Bob Hope, comedian	boxer
Boris Karloff, actor	real estate salesman
Elvis Presley, singer	truck driver

> Don't get mad, get even.
> — ADVICE GIVEN TO LEE IACOCCA BY HIS WIFE, MARY,
> AFTER HE WAS FIRED FROM HIS JOB OF THIRTY-TWO YEARS AT FORD

Coke changed their successful formula and launched New Coke. What a disaster that was. But they reacted quickly and reintroduced Coke Classic. They recovered so well that pundits wondered, "Did they plan it that way?"

I received one very negative book review for *Leadership from Within*. Instead of ignoring it, I treated it as a gift and mailed out the following announcement. People loved it.

— PETER

When Adversity Hits,
Remember What Was Said About . . .

The Beatles. Decca Recording Co. said:
"We don't like their sound, and guitar music is on the way out."

Fred Astaire. An MGM testing director said:
"Can't act. Slightly bald. Can dance a little."

Vince Lombardi, the famous football coach. An expert said:
"He possesses minimal football knowledge. Lacks motivation."

Ludwig van Beethoven. His music teacher called him:
hopeless as a composer.

Enrico Caruso, the famous opera singer. His teacher said:
he had no voice at all and could not sing.

Albert Einstein. One teacher described him as:
mentally slow, unsociable, and adrift forever in his foolish dreams.

Rodin, the famous Renaissance sculptor. His father said:
"I have an idiot for a son."

Leo Tolstoy, author of *War and Peace*. He was described as:
both unable and unwilling to learn.

Peter Urs Bender. About his best-selling book, *Leadership from Within*, one reviewer said:
*"Suffers from an annoying lack of substance . . .
This disastrous book . . . should be avoided."*

As **Winston Churchill** once said, in the face of adversity:
"Never, never, never, never give up."

---

www.PeterUrsBender.com

USING THE POWER OF CREATIVITY

> If you believe you are creative,
> you are.

> Companies are increasingly falling into two categories
> — those that are innovative and those that go out of business.
> — *DAN BRANDA, CEO, HEWLETT-PACKARD CANADA*

A company should never be satisfied with its products and services. Hewlett-Packard, known for its innovative printing technology, began with $500 in cash and has exceeded $25 billion in sales.

Creativity is a learned skill that ranks with communication as one of the two most important skills for success in the new millennium. You may have heard that we live in the information age. You may also have heard that "information is power." That is not true! *Information is not power. The power is in the application of information.* Having all the information about your customer's likes and dislikes and your competition's offerings is not power by itself — it simply has power potential, until you exploit your knowledge creatively.

In the game of chess each player has equal information. Each can see the same board and knows all the previous moves. The player who makes better use of the information is the one who wins.

In her book *Shifting Gears*, economist Nuala Beck described the cheap and abundant commodity that fuelled each era of the economy. The abundance and affordability of steel fuelled the industrial age, while oil did the same for the energy age. Information is the cheap and abundant commodity of the present day.

In today's marketplace, you and your competition may be working with the same information, since access is almost unrestricted. So how do you add more value? By being creative! That can give you the edge, get you noticed, get you more marketing exposure — which translates into more business.

SCAMPER

You can force yourself to think differently, to come up with and implement crazy ideas by using the SCAMPER system. SCAMPER is an acronym created by Bob Eberle to apply the lessons of creative advertising genius Alex Osborn.

> Substitute
> Combine
> Adapt
> Modify, Minimize, Maximize
> Put to another use
> Eliminate, Erase
> Reverse, Rearrange

As you can see, SCAMPER is a checklist of idea-generating actions to be applied to a product, a system, or a concept. When you are focusing on creativity, come up with as many crazy ideas as you can — and then stretch some more. The creative process is most effective when you first get all ideas out on the table, uncensored. Later you can review them for practicability. Here are some ways to use SCAMPER in your brainstorming work:

Substitute

Replace one of the components of your product with some other material. Automotive manufacturers substituted plastic for metal to reduce weight and improve mileage. They are now substituting further with lighter, stronger steel. Look at the construction industry, where studs are now made of metal instead of wood and pipes are made of plastic instead of metal.

Combine

Combine two or more concepts that do not normally go together. Centuries ago, the Earl of Sandwich slapped a piece of meat on a slice of bread and created the sandwich. Johann Gutenberg changed the world when he combined a wine press with a coin stamp, creating the first printing press and lauching the information age. Walk down the soup aisle at the grocery store and you'll see some other unusual combinations.

Adapt

Take an idea and make it work for you in a different context. Zenon Environmental adapted nature's principle of osmosis to create a water purification system that would be sold around the world.

A Swiss inventor discovered the principle of hooks and loops by observing how burrs clung to clothing, then adapted that to create Velcro. Velcro was the answer to the space program's question, "How will the astronauts fasten their outfits with those big gloves on?" Velcro was later adapted to help the parents of preschoolers, who asked, "How do we get our kids to fasten their shoes?"

Henry Ford adapted the principle of the production line to automotive production. He reported that he got the idea from the overhead trolley system used by Chicago meat packers in dressing beef. As the carcass moves along the trolley, subsequent cuts are made until nothing is left. He just reversed the process and applied it to cars.

Many individuals who are downsized learn to adapt their corporate skills as entrepreneurs. The surfboard was adapted for use on land as a skateboard and later influenced the design of the snowboard. Ad signs are displayed in public washrooms. Magazine publishing principles are easily adapted to producing web pages on the Internet.

Modify, Minimize, Maximize

Consider simply changing the size or shape of your product. Chrysler launched the successful minivan by making vans a little smaller. Retail was revitalized by the advent of "big-box" stores such as the Price Club and Home Depot. The radio industry maximizes news content by launching twenty-four-hour news stations.

The blossoming investment market is the result of people attempting to maximize their retirement wealth. Health and beauty services and products promise to minimize the effects of aging.

The tee in T-ball that allows young children to enjoy baseball is an overgrown golf tee.

Put to Another Use

After SPAR Aerospace sold NASA all the Canadarms that were needed, they looked around for another market. They put their arm to another use by selling it as a backhoe for use by the U.S. military in cleaning up old missile silo sites.

I remember watching the TV show *MacGyver* to see what new uses the lead character could create for duct tape. In my seminars on creative problem solving I sometimes challenge the participants to find 100 uses for duct tape.

Erase, Eliminate

Take out the parts that don't add value. Food companies do this by offering caffeine-free, reduced-salt, and sugarless versions of their products. Eliminate excess packaging to reduce costs and environmental waste. Remove annoying administrative steps from your sales procedures. A buyer for a medium-sized institution told me they achieved a better price than a much larger buyer because they eliminated unnecessary paperwork in the transaction.

Reverse, Rearrange

Try reversing perceptions. Which came first, the microscope or the telescope? One is just the reverse of the other.

The banks reversed the responsibility of who does their service work. They train customers to use the automated teller machines and process their own transactions. Did they learn this idea from the gasoline "service" stations that did the same thing to their customers decades earlier?

Most retailers built warehouses to serve existing retail outlets. Sam Walton, founder of Wal-Mart, reversed the method by starting with a giant warehouse, then building stores around it. This resulted in a more cost-effective supply system which enabled lower retail prices.

Send us your examples. We may publish them in the next edition. (See the appendix for how to contact us.)

USING SCAMPER FOR CREATIVE MARKETING

To find new ideas for your marketing program, write a detailed list of your current marketing efforts. Then for each strategy, apply each of the SCAMPER actions. Be very specific, and add details that describe the physical attributes and methods of your marketing materials and actions.

Here is a simple example for one part of a marketing program:

Current effort: I mail post cards to my A clients and media contacts when I travel to exotic places.

Using SCAMPER, this strategy has all kinds of possibilities. Consider:

Substituting unusual gifts for post cards
Substituting any far-away places for exotic places
Substituting phone calls for mail
Combining business and personal travel
Combining the mailing list with that of another company
Adapting by sending regular note cards
Adapting by sending e-mail post cards
Adapting by sending custom-printed post cards
Modifying the mailing list
Modifying the design of the post cards
Maximizing by finding the largest post card
Maximizing the mailing to get in the Guinness Book of World Records
Putting book covers to *another use* as post cards
Putting flying time to *another use* by writing the post cards
Eliminating the cost of postage by finding a sponsor
Eliminating the use of post cards because everyone does it
Reversing the sequence by writing the postcards after returning home, then mailing them in bulk to a colleague who will post from the exotic location
Reversing the thinking by getting clients to mail me post cards.

The purpose of SCAMPER is to generate a lot of ideas. Then play with them, pick the best ones, and apply them. Some ideas look crazy at first but may later hit you like an "ah-ha!" when you're in a position to implement them.

> He who thinks you are crazy
> is just different from you.

Now you can try the SCAMPER method to liven up one of your marketing approaches. Write a statement from your marketing plan. Then create a list of possibilities. Here are some tips to get you going:

Substitute

What can you substitute? A different medium, material, content, spokesperson, plastic business card, a woman wearing a tux instead of a fancy dress . . .

Combine

What can you combine — a joint promotion with another company, a bundling of your services, a partnership . . . ?

Should you combine your efforts with another company to share costs of a trade show or publicity campaign, or to help market each other?

Jennifer Kubilis of Hamilton, Ontario, is a bookkeeper who gave her business card impact by spending one cent more. Her slogan is "Bookkeeping solutions that make cents." Glued to each and every card is one shiny penny.

Adapt

What can you adapt — a concept used for a completely different product, a lesson from: nature, history, a song, a movie theme, a TV show, your competitor, another industry . . . ?

Can you adapt a successful product theme to a new line? Can you enter a new market by adapting your product to a different client culture?

Modify, Minimize, Maximize

What can you modify, make smaller, or make larger — the smallest mascot, the largest sign, the shortest response time, a cheque printed on a large board . . . ?

Can you modularize your service? Can you offer an introductory, intermediate, and advanced level? Can you minimize your risk by negotiating early payment?

Put to Another Use
Can you find a new use for an antique, use a balloon to explain your concept, use a kids' toy as a calling card . . . ?

How can you put customer product returns to another use? Could you donate them to a charity? How can you put customer complaints and compliments to another use? Could you use them in a news release? How can you put your hobby to another use? Could you make it part of a promotional event? How can you put to another use that awful piece of art you received as a gift? Give it to some distant relative? (Just kidding.)

Erase, Eliminate
Find a big pain or annoyance, then eliminate it. The biggest pain might be the way everyone else does business in this industry. This is why customer complaints are so valuable. They are gems because they help generate new products, new methods, and new markets.

How's this for a process of elimination:

eliminate the risk: offer a 100 or 110 percent
  money-back guarantee
eliminate the paperwork: do it electronically
eliminate the breakdown: offer regular maintenance
eliminate the cost: get a sponsor
eliminate the distance: move closer
eliminate some of the costs: use technology
eliminate inventory: use "just-in-time" shipping
eliminate waste: manufacture to quality standards
eliminate incorrect orders: make it simple

Reverse, Rearrange
Reverse the usual perception. Listen instead of talking. Make it easy for your customers instead of efficient for you. Give away something free in

an industry that normally charges high rates. Offer services *à la carte* when your competitors force customers to buy a whole package.

REVERSING

When McDonald's prepared to open its first restaurant in Moscow, the company had to make a critical decision on what currency to accept. This was in the early days of perestroika. The USSR was hungry for hard currency — anything Western. Rubles could not be exchanged for foreign currency. Special state-owned Beriozka shops sold all kinds of food and goods, but did not make them available to the local population. Each of these government shops displayed a brass sign out front that virtually shouted, in Russian, "Hard Currency Only."

McDonald's decided to accept rubles. It was the only way to reach the locals. On the front door of the McDonald's restaurant was a similar brass sign displaying the words, in English and Russian, "Rubles Only."

The locals loved it. What a way to build customer loyalty. And all the papers ran the story.

> When you come to a fork in the road — take it.
> — *YOGI BERRA*

PERSIST

Ideas start as seeds — at first they're always fragile and imperfect. Edison laboured over 10,000 attempts before his light bulb came to be. The first form of your idea will likely be flawed. You must not get discouraged by others who put you down. Instead, avoid sharing ideas with those people. You must care for and nurture your creations.

HAVE FUN

Humour is a powerful tool for spurring creativity. If you can laugh about a difficult situation, you may find that you can come up with some really wild solutions. Sometimes desperation forces us to throw up our hands and think outside the lines.

Children laugh at a lot of things adults don't find funny. At times, we get upset at them, but there is no question that children are more creative than adults. Unfortunately, parents and the school system tend to teach children to conform, to stop acting silly, to come up with "the answer." In most cases, there is no one answer. Think like the kid you once were, and have some fun. Ask yourself silly questions. You may discover some truly unique solutions to your grown-up problems.

Ask yourself "Why?" to broaden your thinking and uncover new approaches. Ask "What if?" to play with new ideas. And enjoy yourself.

For more creative resources, see the appendix.

ZIG WHEN ALL ELSE ZAG

If you want to be noticed, you've got to be different. Find out what everybody else does — then do something different.

Everyone sends Christmas cards. You send Ground Hog Day cards.
Everyone sends brochures. You send post cards.
Everyone makes an appointment. You just show up.
Everyone goes through Human Resources. You go to the President.
Everyone screens their calls. You answer your own phone.
Everyone wears a regular tie. You wear a bow tie.
Everyone has their photo on their card. You have your logo.
Everyone sends flowers. You send plants.
Everyone sends their material on the last day. You deliver it early.
Everyone has a fax machine. You have fax on demand.

Get the picture?

Write down ten things that everyone does in your industry. Then put your own twist on them. You don't have to use every one. They are just ideas to get you thinking of ways to be different.

Any fool can make a rule and every fool will mind it.
— *HENRY DAVID THOREAU*

CHANGE THE RULES

We all live by rules. Rules are good. They are the results of experience and lessons learned, and they can save us time and money and keep us from harm.

Rules also restrict options. That's why they can be both good and bad. "Look all ways before crossing the street" is a good rule that we learn as kids and pass on to our own children. "Stop when you come to a red light" is another good rule. But who would be dogmatic enough to force an emergency vehicle to wait for the green? There are necessary exceptions to every rule.

Most rules start with good intentions, but situations change. Many police forces once had minimum weight and height requirements for their officers. The theory was that police officers had to be big, strong, and threatening in appearance. In the days of the Wild West, when marshals worked alone on vast stretches of land, that was probably a good theory. But in modern times, such regulations precluded the hiring of women and some people of nationalities that tend to be smaller in stature. With advanced mental and physical training, modern technology, and new attitudes, the rules have changed, and our police forces are more diverse and representative of the population at large.

The rules of business can also restrict options. They are usually created by the market leaders. But remember that if you follow *their rules* you are playing *their game* — one you probably cannot win.

Mostly these rules are unwritten. If you are new to an industry, you can either follow the rules and follow the pack, or change the rules and lead. The latter approach often creates controversy, which may earn you lots of free publicity.

The unwritten rules are the hardest to change, because they are not always evident. We often follow unwritten rules subconsciously and without question. But if we become more aware of them, we can see them as opportunities for change.

To discover the unwritten rules in your industry, describe the process of doing business in your market in detail. For every detail, ask the question "Why?" Whenever the answer is, "We've always done it this way," alarm bells should go off. You have found a potential opportunity to change.

Dell Computers changed the rules in the computer-selling game. Instead of selling to distributors who in turn sold to the consumer, Dell sold directly to consumers by mail order. They were not the first business to sell by mail order. But they were the first to apply the idea to personal computers.

Amazon.com changed the rules of bookselling by setting up shop on the Internet. Now every time an expert talks or writes about the Internet, they mention Amazon.com — that adds up to tons of free exposure.

All rules are based on perceptions.
As things change the rules become outdated.

Henry Ford challenged the rules of the automotive marketplace with his proclamation, "I will build a motorcar for the great multitude." Until then the automobile had been a status symbol handcrafted for the rich only.

Ford dropped the price of the Model T from $575 in 1912 to $99 in 1914. Profits fell initially, but soon sales exploded; market share rose from 9.4 percent in 1909 to 48 percent in 1914. Profits followed.

Charles Merrill, cofounder of Merrill Lynch, shocked the investment world in 1947 by offering stocks and bonds to the middle class! Imagine how the rich felt.

Ignoring market research, Ted Turner launched the Cable News Network, CNN, in 1980. No one thought a twenty-four-hour news network would work. It did.

CHANGING THE RULES

Visiting the dentist is supposed to be painful — everybody knows that. The first time I visited my new dentist he surprised me, not with a shiny new drill, but by his manner.

He was casually dressed, without the usual lab coat. He introduced himself with "Hi, I'm Ralph" instead of calling himself "Doctor so and so." First we chatted — before he looked inside my mouth — so that I could talk without my mouth full of his fingers and equipment. One of the facts that came out in the conversation was that he enjoyed scuba diving — something I had always wanted to do. We both had a keen interest in photography. On my second visit he proudly showed me his album of underwater photographs.

Guess what? I like this dentist. It would be very difficult to get me to switch to someone else. I used to have a fear of dentists because I had a lot of fillings and pain when I was younger. By changing the unwritten rule that dentists must act and appear clinical and aloof, this dentist changed my attitude, and gained a loyal customer.

— *GEORGE*

good to pano for 12wks

To receive your own free sign like this, place an order by visiting www.Torok.com.

FLEXIBILITY

One of the greatest advantages that small business has over large corporations is flexibility. You don't need to call a meeting, send your ideas to the steering committee, form a task force, or take a vote on new strategies. You are a sailboat, while the big corporation is an oil tanker. You need to stay out of the way of the oil tanker, but what you do with your little boat is your call — and you can change tack quickly.

As an example, consider the story of Francis Drake. He defeated the overwhelmingly superior fire power of the Spanish Armada because he broke the rules and capitalized on his own fleet's flexibility. Drake was a pirate by trade, so instead of standing off at a distance and trading broadsides with his foe, as was the custom of military action at the time, he darted among their fleet. His smaller, lighter ships moved so quickly the Spanish galleons could not hit them. They were more likely to hit their own fleet. Drake fired, then moved on and fired again. He broke all the rules, but he saved England and Queen Elizabeth I knighted him.

❙ The only rule is, there are no rules.

Let's do a quick recap of the ways you can leverage your marketing by capitalizing on what's already out there. You might wish to think of these tips as the "3Rs of Marketing" — reuse, recycle, repackage.

Reuse
- reprint article
- reproduce your successful ideas, articles, events, products
- borrow ideas from others
- sell a different product to existing customers
- turn events in the news into media exposure
- recruit customers for referrals to new prospects

Recycle
- look for ideas from other industries
- slice, dice, and remix an old program
- bring back an old theme from history
- ask for ideas from your colleagues, customers, and staff
- break rules — and make new ones
- turn obstacles into positives
- transform defeats into learning points
- change complaints into new products and services
- piggy-back on well-known names by licensing or partnering

Repackage
- cut and paste articles

- combine customer testimonials on one page
- deliver the product by a different method
- change your look
- form a virtual team for a big project
- have a professional edit your materials
- offer a product to a new market
- change the image through repositioning
- find a business use for your hobbies
- change your message to emphasize different features of your product

4.4 LEVERAGING TOOLS

Now that you're thinking about how to creatively leverage your assets, strengths, weaknesses, experiences, and ideas into Power Marketing, you're ready to choose your tools. The following ideas will show you more specific ways to focus, to be unique, and to be creative using the 3Rs. Use what works for you and add some of your own. Then send them to us and we will add them to our list and periodically send you an updated Power Marketing Hottest Tips list.

YOUR ARTICLES

After you publish an article in a paper or magazine, you need to let everyone know about it. You can do that in two ways, either by sending out originals of the whole publication or by sending out copies of the article. (You can even cut and paste copies of your letters to the editor, if they are informative or entertaining.)

SEND THEM THE WHOLE MAGAZINE

Get extra copies of the publication. Ask for as many free copies as you can get. Some will give you only a handful, while others may give you hundreds of copies. If your article looks really good and/or it is a prestigious magazine, buy many more.

Send these copies to your clients and prospects. They will be more impressed if you send them the whole magazine, especially if it is one they might enjoy reading. Make it easy for them to find your article by marking it with a post-it flag (and don't forget to mark any pages where your article is "continued.") On the front cover place a post-it note saying "Bob, you might enjoy the ten tips on Power Marketing on page 21." Sign your name to it.

Be sure to use your client's name, to catch their attention, and your name, to help them remember you.

Type your name in big bold letters on address labels. Omit your address — just show your name. Place these labels on the front cover of the magazine. If they leave the magazine lying around, anyone who sees the magazine will see your name.

CUT AND PASTE

If you only get a few copies from the publisher of the magazine, then "cut and paste." You should also do this with your newspaper articles, because it's awkward to mail out entire newspapers.

Neatly cut out the article you wrote, being careful to remove the other articles and advertisements that surround it. They distract from what you want the reader to see. Then paste your article on one page. If you have no talent for this, find someone who can do it for you.

Along with the article you must include:

- the magazine or newspaper banner (preferably from the front page)
- the date published (if it is new); on old material, omit the date
- your name
- your phone number
- your e-mail address

You might also include:

- your logo
- your photo (even if it did not appear in the publication)
- a graphic that illustrates the message

This type of communication looks best when you type, rather than hand-write, the date and name of the publication in which your article appeared. Try to get it all on one letter-sized page (8 1/2" x 11"). Use legal-sized paper only if you must.

If the article is short, enlarge the print with the photocopier. This makes it easier to read and it looks more important.

You might not be able to get a clear photocopy of a newspaper or magazine page because of a shaded background, show-through from the reverse side of the original, or faded ink. In that case, retype your article and reprint it on plain paper (or you could ask the publication for a better copy or a master for copying). Then paste on the identifying logo and name of the publication.

Once you have a professional-looking master, run copies on good paper. Use a coloured paper — it looks better than plain white. Textured paper is also a good idea. Run more copies than you think you need; you will always find uses for extras.

Highlight the important points in your article. Remember that even though you love the article, your prospects might only glance at it, so make it easy to find your best point. If you were only one of several experts quoted in an article, highlight your part. Many won't read the article, but they will still say they liked it.

GIVE THEM WIDE DISTRIBUTION

Mail to your clients, prospects, other media, and associations. This is a nice way of keeping your name in front of them without appearing pushy. You are giving them value by sending them the article. In the process they "happen" to notice that you were published yet again, and that builds on your image as an expert.

Be sure to send your published articles to all the media. When other media receive your articles, you look more credible and more newsworthy. In the media everyone watches everyone to make sure they don't miss anything. The media reuse and recycle articles, news, and interviews. If they see something in print in another newspaper or magazine, they may reprint it or rewrite it from a different angle. You may wish to suggest a different angle yourself.

When mailing to associations or companies that have newsletters, include a note: "Let me know if you want to reprint this article in your newsletter." Plant the seed — don't hope that they will come up with the idea on their own. Then call to ask if they do want to use the article. Give them permission — for free — as long as they include your name, phone number, and photo or logo, and on the condition that they provide you with copies. If the publication has a small circulation, ask for a dozen copies; if they normally print thousands of copies, ask for hundreds. Then send the reprinted article out to your prospects all over again. At the same time, add the article to the portfolio that you send to new prospects.

ARTICLES YOU DIDN'T WRITE

When you find articles that support your message or ideas, clip them. Cut and paste them, as described above, and make copies. You might include them in your next mailing package. Or, if an article is timely, send it by itself. Highlight the key point and handwrite, "I agree." This is especially effective if the article is quoting someone like Bill Gates, Albert Einstein, or Helen Keller. By stating that you agree, you are also implying that they agree with you.

Show that you listen to your client's concerns by clipping and sending articles that interest them. When you see your client in the news, call or send them the article with a note of congratulations.

Let us never negotiate out of fear,
but never fear to negotiate.
— JOHN F. KENNEDY

NEGOTIATION

Leverage is about getting more with just a little. Powerful negotiation is an effective way to do this, whether you are negotiating for T-shirts on a beach in Mexico, for extra ad space in a magazine, or for a multi-million-dollar deal. And it is one of the tools you need for Power Marketing.

The three key qualities that will grant you negotiating power are confidence, an ability to listen, and a willingness to walk away from a deal. If you *have* to close a deal to pay the rent, you will be a weak negotiator. If you fail to listen, you will miss key words that tell you what your opponent really wants. If you lack an outward show of confidence, they will see that you are weak and crush you.

When you negotiate you must believe in the value that you offer. Your prospect will see, feel, and hear any doubts. Always negotiate from power. Never beg for business. If a salesperson were begging for your business, how would you react?

GET MORE FOR YOUR BOTTOM LINE

"Negotiation is the way to rewrite your bottom line," says David Webb of Negotiation Resource International (NRI). Webb, based in the U.K., is an international trainer and consultant in negotiation. "Most people negotiate based on instinct and their culture." Often they lack formal training in negotiation. NRI helps companies by coaching them to approach critical negotiations with structure and skill.

There are five basic methods of negotiation used around the world; some are more prevalent in certain cultures, although in today's global economy you will encounter surprises if you count on generalizations.

1. *Compromise*

   This method involves searching for the middle ground. It can be recognized by statements like "Let's split the difference." Webb admits that the British have been known as world-class compromisers. But he sees that changing. Compromise may be the fastest way to reach a conclusion, but the downside is that it involves only one dimension (usually price), on which both parties have to give up something.

2. *Bargaining*

   Bargaining is similar to compromise. But rather than focusing on one issue, two or more options are traded. For example: "If you reduce the price, I will pay sooner." This can become complex with the addition of factors such as delivery, payment terms, service level, repeat orders, quantity, and contract length. Bargaining is common in North America. It can be relatively quick, but, like compromise, it requires both parties to relinquish something. This is not the case with the next three negotiating styles, which are based on threat, logic, and emotion.

3. *Threat*

Threat is most powerful when it is implied. The party in a position of power can issue an ultimatum. When IBM was *the* dominant computer company they could have easily threatened customers: "If you don't buy from IBM, what will your boss say when something goes wrong?" A successful threat involves concessions by only one party. You may choose to use a threat, if you are in a position of power, but beware: threats often backfire. The other party might call your bluff, and you will be required to follow through with actions you never intended to take. It's also advisable to never threaten directly; let the message be implied instead.

4. *Logic*

It is hard to resist the logical argument that a price increase is necessary because of increases in production costs. When one party presents well-researched numbers and logic, the other party does the moving. Generally speaking, Swedes and Germans are most comfortable using this approach. Only emotion can deflect logic.

5. *Emotion*

Children use emotion all the time when negotiating with their parents: "You don't love me anymore." Many believe that emotion has no place in business, but it is actually an effective tactic for getting the other party to move. Latin Americans are known to use emotion extremely well in negotiations. The key is to control your emotions while exploring those of the other party. Some examples: "My boss will kill me if I accept that." "I really need your help to make this work." We also use emotion when we wave the flag: "You want to support the local economy, don't you?"

Nellie McCracken, representing NRI in North America, says that "the secret to successful negotiation is *moving* people." She adds, "It is important to understand and practise all five styles." Negotiation is a skill that can be, no *must* be, learned.

The most powerful negotiating tool is silence.
After you make your offer, pause and smile.

SHARING TOOLS

What if you want to get your marketing materials printed at the 100,000-flyer rate but can't afford to buy that many? Consider finding three other complementary businesses, designing one flyer that lists all four of you, and then splitting the costs so you each get 25,000 flyers for a modest price.

If you call yourself the "Cadillac" of your business, then partner with a Cadillac dealer — or directly with GM. Strike a deal so that every buyer of a Cadillac from your local dealer gets one of your products, or every one of your customers gets a chance to win a draw for a Cadillac.

Find out where your customers shop, then partner with those places for cross promotion. Try clothing shops, restaurants, office supply stores, entertainment venues, car dealerships, health clubs, golf clubs, hotels, travel agents, and so on.

Ask the business you partner with to:

- display a sign describing your services
- show you as a sponsor
- list your phone number
- use your products as a prizes
- offer a free sample
- package your product with their sale
- collect referrals

Add your own ideas . . .

LICENSING

Licensing is a form of franchising that has benefits for both the licensee and the licensor.

LICENSEE

You might become licensed by a larger, more established organization to sell their products, apply their methods, or train using their materials. When you are licensed in this way you gain the credibility of the big organization. This reduces the risk to your clients because they believe they are dealing with a reputable firm, even if they've never heard of you. You also save the time of developing a product by adding an established product to your repertoire. You will feel more confident because you know it works; that makes it easier for you to sell. When clients ask for customer references you can use the references of others who sell the same system. When you are licensed it is only natural that you can charge more.

For example, if you were an independent consultant licensed by Franklin Covey, of Stephen Covey fame, you would have a big edge over an unknown independent consultant. You could just walk in to your client's office with Covey's book, *The Seven Habits of Highly Effective People* — and you'd have instant credibility.

Be very careful about spending a lot of money on unproven programs. The reason you buy a license or franchise is because it is proven, has less risk than your own program, and has a more assured return. A McDonald's franchise will cost you seven figures, but you know it works.

LICENSOR

You might approach licensing from the other direction. You can license your products, program, or services to others. There may be revenue flow from this, but there are even more important benefits. Number one is the boost to your credibility. You must be good if others are out there selling your program. And your name is being used more often. If people hear that you have licensed practitioners, they are likely to be impressed. "Wow! I didn't know you were that big!"

You might consider partnering with a company that is located far away. You license them to sell your product in their location and they license you to sell their products in your locale.

Licensing is one way to grow your distribution network rapidly. If you are selling a product that is time sensitive, rapid distribution is essential.

There are many ways of structuring licensing agreements. It's best, of course, to put even informal agreements in writing, so that both sides understand what is promised. The most important thing is having the right fit. If you don't like, trust, and want to work with a potential partner, don't do it. The best legal contracts in the world don't save you the pain of bad relationships.

During the 1970s, Japanese giant Matsushita developed VHS video and decided to license the technology. Sony developed the superior Betamax but failed to license it. Today the world standard is VHS and Betamax is history.

In 1981 Bill Gates decided to license MS-DOS to IBM, while IBM ceded control of the licence for all non-IBM PCs. This laid the foundation for Microsoft's huge success and IBM's fall from grace.

Ray Kroc did not invent McDonald's. He discovered Mac and Dick McDonald's stand in San Bernardino, California. He opened his franchised restaurant in 1955 and formed McDonald's Corp. Kroc took what he found and from that built the global fast-food company — now with over 25,000 outlets worldwide.

PAY FOR SERVICE

When you start your own business, by necessity you begin by doing all the work yourself. At some point you find yourself doing tasks that you should be paying someone else to do. You will get a higher return on your time (greater leverage on your limited resources) if you are are free to do more strategic, higher-value work. You may not need to hire staff; perhaps you could pay a fee for service as required. Corporations call this outsourcing.

FINDER'S FEE

Want to recruit dozens of part-time sales people who only get paid when they deliver, without the hassle of hiring and firing? Offer a finder's fee to those who refer business to you. Make it worth their while and pay them even if it's unclear whether their referral or your own networking resulted in the connection. Make this offer to colleagues, suppliers, past clients, your banker, lawyer, dentist, hairdresser, and so on.

Offer two types of finder's fee: one for referrals and another, more attractive reward for a referral that results in business for you. For example, you might offer a book or lottery ticket for referrals, but $50 or $100 cash when the finder's referral becomes a paying customer.

TURN ALL YOUR STAFF INTO SALES AND MARKETING PEOPLE

Your employees will act according to your example and the actions you reward or punish. If you complain about their work not getting done while they were helping a customer, they'll stop helping customers.

Reward your staff for bringing in new business and new clients. Give cash, recognition, theatre tickets, or a special award.

Fifth Avenue Collection, a direct fashion jewellery seller, presents each hostess of an in-home product showing with a unique piece of jewellery. This special gift is not for sale — it is reserved exclusively for hostesses. The real cost remains a mystery and the value of the gift is enhanced because it is special. The strategy also encourages others to host an in-home showing.

In the same way, Super Bowl rings can only be obtained by winning the big game. You can't buy one, so they are tremendously valuable.

VOLUNTEERING

How is volunteering a marketing tool? First let me explain the leveraging effect. You volunteer to help with a cause. The measure of success is achieving the goal of the project or moving closer to the vision of the cause. The bonus (this is where the leverage comes in) is that you have increased visibility in the form of press coverage, stronger relationships, wider networks, enhanced credibility, and growth in your people skills. You are seen doing something good, and people like that; they may be more likely to want to do business with you.

"I'm so busy, I don't have time to volunteer," you say. Okay. If you don't have time you don't have time. But you'll find that if you can squeeze in a few hours a month, or several hours in certain months, you will benefit because it feels good to help someone else. Volunteering always pays off in several ways — all of them better than money. Pick a cause you truly believe in. Don't volunteer just because you think it's good marketing, even though it often is.

SUSTAINABLE DEVELOPMENT

During my early speaking days I volunteered for my city's Sustainable Development Committee. I was passionate about the balance between economy, environment, and society. I learned a lot and contributed significantly. I met many local citizens and learned about how the city functioned. My effort and results stood me in good stead when I dealt with the same people later in other capacities — and when I needed their help.

Because of my work on the committee I had many opportunities to speak. The one I remember best is for my son's Grade 4 class. I anguished about how I would explain a term like sustainable development to them. To my delight they were a bright and eager class and I had fun. A few days later my son brought home a large envelope addressed to me. Upon opening it and unfolding the contents I discovered the best and largest thank-you note I ever received. It was printed on two large sheets of flip-chart paper and signed by all the students in the class. That note was worth more

than all the fancy letters I've ever received.

Later a friend suggested I use my big thank-you note for marketing. I pasted the two sheets on the wall and took a picture of me standing beside it. Then I photocopied the picture and included it in my portfolio. That was part of the information package that later won me the chance to design and teach a college course on environmental purchasing to a group of entrepreneurs.

— *George*

Volunteering is a great way to meet people who might not ordinarily talk to you. You get to work with them as an equal and they will remember you when and if you knock on their door for business.

If you choose to run a volunteer program you can approach the rich and mighty and ask for their help in terms of money, time, resources, or testimonials of support. These might be people you do not normally meet. Once you have made contact with these influential people, stay in touch. Start by sending them one of your articles.

JOB SEEKERS' SEMINAR

Years ago I decided to organize a non-profit seminar to help job seekers in a tough job market.

I asked the mayor for his written endorsement. He already knew me from my volunteer work with the Sustainable Development Committee, so he agreed. He signed a letter on his official letter-head praising the seminar and encouraging job seekers to attend. (I wrote the letter for him.)

With official support for my seminar, I sent copies of that letter to the media. That resulted in some free ads and an interview on local television. And the local cable television station attended my seminar and taped the whole program.

My volunteer work gave me credibility with the mayor. The mayor's endorsement gave me credibility with the media. This in turn gave the seminar additional appeal in the public's eyes. The success of the program gave me still more credibility with the media and the seminar market.

— *GEORGE*

I cannot live without books.
— *THOMAS JEFFERSON, LETTER TO JOHN ADAMS, JUNE 10, 1815*

BOOKS

If you write a book, it can become a powerful marketing tool. But if you aren't a published author, you can still use books for your marketing.

Give books as gifts. Those who read will love it. Those who do not read will remember you. They will keep the book on the shelf. They may throw away a lot of paper and brochures, but they're likely to hang on to books.

Sign Re Workbook

YOUR OWN BOOK

Give it away — to clients, media, and prospects. A book is far better than a business card because it's harder to lose or file away.

More than anything else, your own book labels you as "the" expert. And don't forget that a book signed by the author is made more valuable. Sign it!

Leverage this valuable asset by using your book as:

- your business card
- your service flyer
- your proposal
- your résumé
- a gift for business-card draws
- a thank-you gift to clients
- a thank you for referrals
- a door opener to prospects
- a door opener to media
- a reason for media to interview you

I know of some authors who traded copies of their books with a driver for a ride to the airport in the limousine.

If you are being introduced as a speaker, have the introducer hold and display your book to the audience. Make it easier for the introducer by suggesting they read from the book — and have an appropriate introduction printed in large type, double-spaced, *right in the book itself.*

> From the moment I picked up your book until I laid it down I was convulsed with laughter. Some day I intend on reading it.
> — GROUCHO MARX

OTHER BOOKS

Listen to your clients and you will discover their interests, their pain, and their passion. Recommend a book or, even better, give them a book you think they will like. They will remember you every time they open it.

It's okay to give someone a book you didn't write, but the book should be relevant to the recipient's work or lifestyle, or it could be one you use as a reference in your own work. It might be written by the guru of the industry. It might be written by a friend or colleague.

Sign the book on the inside front cover and include a personal message. Insert your card in the book. Place labels in the book with your name, address, and phone number. Signing the book makes it more personal.

If you want the recipient to see an interesting page, mark it with a post-it flag.

> Books are the treasured wealth of the world
> and the fit inheritance of generations and nations.
> — HENRY DAVID THOREAU, WALDEN

AUDIOTAPES

If you have audiotapes of your program or speeches, send them to preferred customers. Busy people listen to audiotapes in their cars. If your tape is good, you have a captive audience.

When you speak at a conference that is being taped, negotiate with the organizers to get free copies of the tape of your session. Send these tapes to your best clients.

When you copy tapes, leave about ten seconds of blank tape at the beginning. Just before you send the tape out, personalize it using those ten seconds. Record a personal greeting from you to your client: "Hi Sue, this is Peter Urs Bender. Hope you enjoy this tape with tips on marketing your business."

When you attend a conference or seminar and hear an impressive speaker, buy extra copies of the tapes. Send those tapes to your special clients with a note: "I found this session to be the best at the conference and thought you would enjoy it too."

Have small labels printed with your name, address, and phone number, and affix them to the tapes you send out. Every time they play the tape they will be reminded that you sent it to them and they'll know how to reach you.

good idea!

> Marketing is not the art of selling. It is the art of creating conditions by which the buyer convinces himself.
> And nothing is more convincing than hard evidence that others want the same thing.
> — HARVEY MACKAY,
> SWIM WITH THE SHARKS WITHOUT BEING EATEN ALIVE

TESTIMONIAL LETTERS

Letters and recommendations from happy clients are very powerful. Testimonials might take the form of a thank you for your good work or a hearty recommendation for your service.

Sometimes you will receive a testimonial letter from a client who raves about your service. Treasure each and every one. If a letter is particularly good, ask the client to make copies for you on their letterhead. That way you have a sharp original to send to your prospects. They may not give you blank letterhead but they may be glad to run the copies for you. Ask for 100 to 500 copies. Tell them you'll pay for the letterhead. If they order their letterhead in large quantities, 500 copies should cost less than $20, but you may find that they won't bother charging you. If you gave them a reduced rate for your work, it would be hard for them to say no to your request for copies. You might even negotiate for a testimonial letter (if and only if they are completely satisfied with your service) when you make the original deal.

If the letter is good but they will not run copies for you, then make your own copies. You have a couple of options, and cost is the determining factor. First, you could have copies run by your offset printer in two colours. Use black for the type. Use blue for the logo and signature. The colour may not be correct for the logo but your prospects won't notice. The signature in blue will stand out from the typed words and look original.

A less costly option is to photocopy (black ink) onto a lightly coloured paper (try grey, blue, or cream). The coloured paper looks more substantial and important than plain white.

HOW TO MAKE THE LETTER MORE INTERESTING

Check the newspaper or the client's internal newsletter or brochures for an interesting headline, blurb, logo, CEO photo, or product photo and cut and paste this onto the letter. Be sure to get copyright permission if you plan to do this for a brochure or large printing.

If the client is praising a speech you gave at a conference, you might cut and paste a list of other high-profile speakers who would enhance your credibility. Bill Gates or Lee Iacocca, of course, would be great. You could cut and paste their photos next to yours under the heading "Guest Speakers." You don't need to list all the speakers — just you and the important ones. Note that by doing this, you are not telling lies; you are simply showing who else spoke at the same event. Again, check with the conference organizers to make sure you have permission to print the photos. If they balk or ask for money, remind them that you are helping to promote their event. In all likelihood, they will gladly accept more "free publicity."

If the letter reads well but is in a bad font or faint type, retype it in an easier-to-read font, then cut and paste onto the letterhead.

If the letter raves about your service but the writer has included an inside joke or inappropriate comment, either retype, omitting the comment, or cut out or cover up the comment with blank paper or "whiteout."

Clients may not send you a letter unsolicited. Ask for the letter when they are thanking you for the great job you did. Respond to their thanks by asking, "Would you do me a big favour and put those exact words in a letter to me?"

Help them write the letter. Send them samples and some tips for writing testimonial letters. Below is a tips list for writing a testimonial for a speaker. You may use it as is or adapt it to your needs.

TIPS ON WRITING A TESTIMONIAL LETTER FOR A SPEAKER

Here are some questions to ask yourself when writing a letter about a speaker:

1. How did you feel when the presentation was over?
2. How effective was the presentation in pursuing your objective as the organizer?

3. What did you gain from this presentation that was helpful to you or your organization?
4. How effective was the speaker's use of props, visuals, humour, and audience participation?
5. What were the speaker's greatest assets?
6. Would you book this speaker again?
7. How could this speaker be useful to other groups?

Now you rework it to apply to your business and write in the appropriate words. Some questions to ask yourself when writing a letter about your _____:

1. *How did you feel* when the _____was over?
2. *How effective* was the _____ in pursuing your objective?
3. *What did you gain* from this _____ that was helpful to you/your organization?
4. *How effective* was the use of _____?
5. What were the *greatest assets* of this _____?
6. *Would you hire* this _____ again?
7. How could this _____be *useful to other groups/companies/individuals?*

Writing a letter takes time and effort, so make it easy for them. Help them by writing and sending them a draft for the letter. All they need to do is make any small changes they wish, transfer it to their letterhead, and send it back to you.

Create a form with a list of comments. All your clients need to do is circle the words that they might use and sign the bottom of the sheet indicating that you have their permission to use their name with the comments.

Once you have obtained a testimonial letter, make it easy for the prospects who'll eventually read it to see the important information. Highlight the really good lines in yellow or some other bright colour. Not everybody will have time to read the whole letter, so make sure they at least glance at the highlights.

Use pieces of the letters. It is not necessary to use the whole letter. You might only use the best comments from the testimonial and add them to your brochure along with the writer's name, title, and company.

CLIENTS' CLIENTS

Ask your clients' clients to give feedback on your services. For example, let's assume the president (your client) hired you to work with his engineers (his staff or "clients"). After the project the engineers loved your work. Ask them to talk to, or, better still, write to the president with their comments. Right after they say, "Wow, that was great," your response could be, "Thank you very much. You know it would really help me a lot if you could write a quick note to your president about my work."

While teaching a six-week course, I handed out feedback sheets to the students every second week. I sent copies of the sheets to the person who had hired me. At the end of the program, when I asked him to write me a testimonial letter, it was easy for him; he simply referred to the feedback sheets from his "clients" — my students.
— *GEORGE*

SPONSORSHIPS

Sponsor a speaker or an information event. This marketing technique is popular among financial-planning companies. They advertise an expert or celebrity speaker and invite their clients and prospects to attend for free. That way they maintain a value-added relationship with their clients and find new ones.

Even if you sponsor someone who speaks for free, you will be listed as the sponsor. No one has to know it didn't cost you real dollars to "sponsor" the speaker. After all, it costs you time and money to make the program happen at all.

Conversely, you may offer to be someone else's guest speaker, and have them sponsor you. You get the free publicity that they generate — and potential new customers.

HOBBIES

Leverage one of your hobbies or interests into an event. A financial planner wanted to do something different for his clients, so he planned a free golf clinic for special clients. He loved golf and he would rather deal with clients who shared his love.

If you are into photography, have a photo contest. If running is your passion, sponsor a 10K run for charity. If you fancy yourself a gourmet chef, have everyone over for a banquet. Whatever you do, make it an event!

The president of a company selling valves and fittings loved ships. He made his passion for ships a part of his business. He bought and refurbished an old trawler, then used it as the international floating showroom for his company. Everywhere the ship docked, the company invited customers and prospects aboard to see the products and enjoy the unique reception.

| You're here to have fun whether you like it or not.

HUMOUR

Humour is a great relationship builder. If you make people laugh, they will remember you — and fondly. If your name sounds funny, acknowledge it when you introduce yourself. They will laugh with you and remember it better. If people are already thinking, "What a funny name," and you admit it yourself, they tend to like you.

Would you rather be known as the serious consultant or the consultant who laughs? (Especially if you are laughing on the way to the bank.) Do you find that the TV commercials you like most are the ones that make you laugh?

A word of caution, however: Don't go around telling jokes. Jokes tend to have the effect of alienating people, or groups of people. Instead, point out what is funny about what you do — or some silly mistake you made.

| Southwest Airlines hires employees based on their sense of humour.

PRESENTATIONS

Speaking to groups can be a great way to become known and to gain credibility. Develop your oral presentation skills. Study the book *Secrets of Power Presentations*, by — guess who? — Peter Urs Bender. Take a seminar on public speaking. Join Toastmasters. Then practise, practise, practise.

Your competition may be bigger and better known than you. But if you can stand and deliver a power presentation, you will outshine them.

I've attended computer shows where senior executives of large well-known computer companies read their speeches — and bored their audiences stiff! If you were in the computer business and happened to present on the same stage, superior presentation skills would be enough to get you noticed. If you are in a technical field you only have to shine a little to stand out among your peers. Not that techies can't give great presentations; it's just that because they are so focused on working with machines and technology, they often neglect their people skills, and end up talking the way they work — using great detail and precision. This can be boring for a non-technical audience. If you are a techie, liven up your speeches with some colourful analogies, smiles, and a conversational manner. Your non-technical audience will appreciate your efforts.

People listen to Bill Gates not because he is a good presenter but because of who he is and the authority he represents. You can compete with the likes of him by being a more powerful presenter.

(Even Bill Gates knew to improve his presentation skills. Before Windows 95 was released Gates studied presentation skills with a few of the top speech coaches in the United States. He is still not the greatest presenter, but he has improved — and he's better than some of his competitors.)

See the chapter "Perceptions" for more about giving speeches and presentations.

GETTING MORE FROM YOUR SPEECH

When you're offered the opportunity to speak, typically you will not be allowed to stand there and just attempt to sell your services for thirty or forty minutes. Your speech must be of value to the group. However, you can still *work in a few mentions of your services*. For example: "We encountered this problem when I was working with a client in the automotive industry and here's how we decided to fix it"; or "When my clients ask me how to approach this problem . . ."; or "That reminds me of the challenge we faced when we helped . . ."

Write your own introduction so your introducer essentially reads a mini-advertisement about you. A good introduction will help your business while building credibility for your speech.

Collect the attendees' business cards. Offer a free draw for a gift or book or coupon. Collect business cards in a hat or box near the end of your speech — maybe just before you close or while you are handling questions — then make the draw and keep the cards. Ask participants to put a check-mark on the back of their cards if they want you to call them about your services. Ask for two checkmarks if they have something urgent they'd like to discuss with you.

Send each attendee a *follow-up* note and offer your services. Call the double-checkmark participants right away — they are your hottest prospects. Call single-checkmark prospects right away too. If some of the other business cards look interesting to you, make a call. The worst that can happen is that the individual tells you he or she is not interested.

Another way to collect business cards is to offer to send a free list of tips to everyone who gives you a card.

> He who asks is a fool for five minutes
> but he who does not ask remains a fool forever.
> — CHINESE PROVERB

ASK QUESTIONS — AND LISTEN

Don't you just hate dealing with big corporations that will not listen to you? Make sure your customers don't feel the same way. Listen to them; in fact, go one better than that — ask them questions and then listen.

Here are some questions you can ask your customers and prospects:

"I am interested in learning about your company's needs. Would you tell me how you evaluated your current supplier?"

"What is the most important issue facing your business in the next five years?"

"Why do your customers buy from you? What makes you different from your competition?"

"Where are you in the marketplace?"

"What is your proudest achievement in the past year?"

Ask customers how they heard about your services, who recommended you, who they've dealt with before, whether or not they were pleased with the previous supplier, what aspect of the current project is most important to them, and so on . . .

Listen carefully to their answers. The information you will glean can be valuable. For example: the client's answer to "how did you hear about us?" will tell you what marketing strategies are working; their responses when you ask about previous suppliers will tell you about the price and level of your competition; and if it's most important to them that the current project is delivered on time, you know not to discount your price — if you deliver promptly, all else will be forgiven.

SEMINARS AND CONFERENCES

When you attend a seminar, conference, or trade show, go with a specific question or purpose in mind. If you know what you are looking for you will find it. These events can be overwhelming, and you may be tempted to act on every idea or piece of information you encounter. Stick to your focus, and make a point of following through on the one thing you wanted to achieve from the outset. It is far better to act on one idea than to write down ten that you won't use.

Be prepared with your 30-second message and business cards. Forget about throwing your cards in the draw prize bowls.

In a seminar you might have the opportunity to ask questions. Stand, state your name and company, and then ask your question. Knowing you will say your name out loud for everyone to hear will force you to think about the question before you ask it. Put a little marketing into it: "I am Leslie Brock, president and founder of Leslie Brock Productions — the fastest-growing web-page creator in [your city]." Then state your question.

CONFERENCES AND CONVENTIONS

There are two keys to learning from others in your industry.

The first is to discover where the best in your business gather to learn. It might be at workshops hosted by your trade association, or at an annual conference. Find out and go. I urge you to do this. Get the money from somewhere. It's an important investment in your business. I would never be where I am in my career if I had not learned from my peers. (In my case, it was at both the "winter workshop" and the annual convention of my trade association.)

The second key is to apply what you learn. When you go to conventions or workshops, you get lots of good ideas. But ideas alone will not improve your business or change your life; progress can only be made when ideas are implemented.

Go where the best are. Learn what works for them. Then follow through and do it.

— *PETER*

> Plans are nothing more than good intentions
> until they are converted into hard work.
> — *PETER F. DRUCKER*

TECHNOLOGY

Technology is a great tool. I don't know how I could run my business if not for voice mail, computers, and the Internet. In addition to the obvious business applications of computers (in areas of accounting, database management, etc.), marketing activities are made cheaper and easier. For example, with laser printers and ink jet printers, you can produce first-class printed material. Commit to learning and relearning how to use your technology. Work it into your schedule. Take a seminar, find an expert, and take time to practise.

Technology can also be a terrible master. I have lost valuable production time over computer problems and shed tears and curses over lost data.

BACKUP SYSTEMS

People often ask me, "What kind of computer should I have for my business?"

My answer is "Two." When they look at me quizzically, I explain, "You are asking the wrong question. It doesn't matter what kind of computer you have — have two of them. One is for backup when the other goes down. And I do mean *when* it goes down — not *if*."

"I can't afford two computers," they say.

"But can you afford to be without your computer for two or three days — maybe longer?"

Remember, computers never misbehave when it is convenient for you. You may not have to have top-of-the-line computers; but it's wiser to have two.

— *PETER*

Fax machines have been around in some form since the 1940s. But only in the 1980s did they catch on. They are still useful. If you find that your clients frequently ask you the same types of questions or request certain lists of information, set up a "fax on demand" system. With fax on demand, a client calls your fax machine, listens to the options, hits the right number, and your machine sends them the information they wanted.

When it comes to getting inexpensive help with your technology, check with the local high school, college, or university for enterprising students. And do not be shy about asking for help.

See the chapters "Perceptions" and "Relationships" for tips on using voice mail, and "Media" for tips on using the Internet and web sites.

4.5 TIME AND LUCK

So far in this chapter, we've seen how you can use any number of tools to leverage your limited resources into Power Marketing techniques. There are two key resources that deserve special attention: *time* and *luck*.

> Dost thou love life?
> Then do not squander time, for that's the stuff life is made of.
> — *BENJAMIN FRANKLIN*

TIME

The beauty about time is that on this dimension, everyone is on equal footing. Everyone has exactly the same hours in a day, in the week, and in the year. It is the most valuable commodity, because you can't buy more at any price. The way to compete on time is to be smarter, not bigger.

The term "time management" is a big fallacy. You can't manage time; you can only manage how you use your time. Here lies a huge opportunity to leverage.

- Show that you respect time — yours and your clients'.
- Schedule all your activities in your daily planning.
- Respond to your clients' inquiries faster than your competition does. (You won't win their business for this alone, but it gives a good impression.)
- Make sure your phone is answered after the first ring.
- Get back to clients on the day they call you.
- Do not waste their time yapping — spend your time listening.
- Separate your leisure time from your work time. When you work, go all out.
- Don't do two-hour lunches — unless it is with a hot prospect.
- Arrange breakfast meetings. They're a great way to start the day (and they're less costly than lunch).
- Send information faster than promised — by fax, e-mail, express mail, or courier.
- Accomplish a great deal before noon and the rest of the day seems a breeze.
- On Fridays, don't quit at noon or two o'clock. Keep on calling and marketing.

| Time is the only non-renewable resource — use it wisely.

It's important to set a schedule for each type of activity related to your business. For example, an effective way to break down a day is as follows:

Prime Time (9:00 a.m.–12:00 p.m. and 2:00–4:00 p.m.)
Spend these hours making cold calls, visiting prospects, and negotiating new business.

Morning Off-Time (6:00–9:00 a.m.)

Use this time for planning and follow-up.

Evening Off-Time (6:00–8:00 p.m.)

Wind down your day with administrative tasks, envelope stuffing, photocopying, etc.

> The only reason for time
> is so that everything doesn't happen at once.
> — *ALBERT EINSTEIN*

Use all of your time, all the time. For example, while on hold on the phone, you can review your notes from a seminar you attended, review your marketing plan, peruse a magazine article, stuff envelopes, or back up computer files. Please don't play solitaire! While driving, you can listen to instructional tapes, check your voice mail (with a hands-free cell phone; safety first!), or rehearse your sales presentation.

Take reading material with you to places where you might need to wait (meetings, the airport, the doctor's office, and so on).

If you join a fitness club, choose one your clients (or other important contacts) might belong to. If you are a runner, use an early-morning run to plan your day, or an end-of-day run to review it.

Writing a letter can take a long time. Consider a change to writing notes — they are faster to write and read, and they're more personal.

Streamline routine tasks. For example, if you have different mailing packages, prepare them ahead of time, in your off hours, so that when a request comes in you have each kind of package at the ready.

Hire others to do the little jobs that you can batch for them. Pay your kids to stuff envelopes, lick stamps, fold paper, affix labels, etc.

Learn to say no. Do not take on too many projects or directions at once. If you have to turn down a job because of time constraints, tell your client why. Then refer the client to a colleague. Both the client and colleague will appreciate your honesty and generosity.

Do less, but spend more time on the things you do well.

> *Time*
> Ever eating, never cloying,
> All-devouring, all-destroying,
> Never finding full repast,
> Till I eat the world at last.
> — *JONATHAN SWIFT,*
> *AUTHOR OF* GULLIVER'S TRAVELS

LUCK

The trick to leveraging luck — the most intangible of resources — is to recognize it when it crosses your path. Luck never shows up when or where you expect it to. Although many of us equate it with a lottery win, luck more often takes the form of a chance meeting, a problem, or a big mistake.

> Success is luck.
> Just ask any loser.

The reality is that if you do enough good things, if you work at them consistently, if you get out and about, and if you keep your head up looking for opportunities and lessons — luck will shine your way. But often it walks in the door disguised and gets ignored.

The business world is filled with good-luck stories.

In 1943, Paul Garret of General Motors asked a young Austrian teacher and writer, Peter Drucker, to study the company. The career of the century's foremost management thinker was launched.

In April 1978, John Larson of McKinsey & Co. asked colleague Tom Peters to step in at the last minute to do a presentation on some research Peters had done. The presentation led to *In Search of Excellence*, which changed the book market and created the management guru industry.

In 1961, Jean Neditch was put on a diet by the obesity clinic at the New York City Department of Health. She invited six dieting friends to meet in her Queens apartment every week. The decision (was it luck?) created Weight Watchers and the slimming industry.

SUMMARY
SECRETS OF LEVERAGE

- Get more impact out of the intangible resources you have, instead of worrying about the tangibles you lack.
- Focus — do more of less. Then position yourself as number one in your defined market.
- Reuse, recycle, and repackage ideas, products, or methods from your competitors, from other industries, or from long ago.
- Break through the unwritten rules that are holding you back. Do it with style and make a big splash.
- Get happy clients to do more for you by asking them to write testimonials. Reproduce their remarks and distribute them with your portfolio, in your newsletter, on your web site.

Show me the names on your database,
and I know who you are.
— Peter Urs Bender

Database Marketing

If the house is on fire,
forget the china, silver, and wedding album —
grab the Rolodex.
— *Harvey Mackay, author of*
Beware the Naked Man Who
Offers You His Shirt

STRATEGY FIVE

In previous chapters, we've explored topics that are inherently interesting: perceptions and relationships, which deal with psychology and people; media, which have a certain cachet; and leverage, which connotes power and movement toward success. Our next inspiring topic is — database marketing!

Does that term bore you? If it does, you're not alone; this is a marketing strategy that doesn't have a high glamour quotient. But we know that if an idea sounds boring to our audience, they're not going to listen. When that happens, we have to change our style, and do whatever is required to give our idea some appeal and make them want to listen.

So we'll do just that. Forget "database marketing." Let's talk about increasing sales to your clients. Finding and keeping prospects who are interested in your work, and may at some time want to buy it. And making it easy for those who love what you do to tell others about it. Put in those terms, doesn't database marketing sound more appealing?

Do you know people who love what you do? If you don't, you should probably get a new line of work! Every worthwhile business has people who love its products and services. The question is, how do you keep it that way? How do you make sure they stay aware of what you're doing and keep valuing your product?

> Be in touch with your clients and prospects on a regular basis.
> Or they forget you!

It's that simple. And that is where "databases" come in. After all, the simplest form of database is an *address book*. A database is just a collection of information. Your business might naturally have several databases: look in your customer files, supplier files, invoice files, product catalogue, and so on.

Remember that information itself is not power; rather, the power is in *how you use* information. That said, the more information you collect about your clients, prospects, and marketplace, the better able you will be to make informed decisions.

Your database can be as small or as large as you like. It can hold your most recent customers or everyone you've ever served. It could have the names of your hot prospects, or everyone who has ever given you their business card! You might include your media contacts, your suppliers, associations you belong to, friends, and relatives.

> On average, each time we experience great service we tell 1.5
> people. But when we get bad service, we're likely to tell seven.

5.1 YOUR DATABASE

I know business owners who track their business expenses and income by keeping twelve envelopes marked January through December. Each month they store their receipts and invoices in the appropriate envelope. At the end of the year they proudly present to their accountant these twelve envelopes. The accountant prepares their annual income tax statement, and then they start the year all over again.

This is a very simple database. It is a system that works, if you only want to look at your status once a year. You could use a similar system for keeping track of your clients and prospects if you only needed to check with them once a year. Would that work? Probably not. Your information about your clients needs to be current — every day of the year. You don't know when they might need you.

Before computers, you would have needed an elaborate paper system for your database. It might have included a Rolodex, business-card file, file cabinet, desk-top hot file, in and out trays, miscellaneous piles of paper, a daily planner, weekly planner, monthly planner, and a wall-mounted year-at-a-glance calendar.

Today you can do all these functions on your computer. You might still use some of these paper systems. In fact I recommend you do maintain some paper systems — as backup to the computer. You might use a day planner, wall calendar, cork board, and/or hot file.

There are several good software programs that can do the job. They are usually known as PIMs (personal information managers), contact managers, customer managers, or calendars. ACT!, Maximizer, and Outlook are just a few of the programs that are available. Look for one that satisfies your needs.

The important point is that you should *use a computer database system*. Don't sacrifice money for a less effective system. This is not the place to buy less than you need.

> Knowing your customers
> is just as important
> as knowing your product.

EXPANDING YOUR ADDRESS BOOK

Suppose you wanted to take your address book and add some notes about each person. Say, for example, you wanted to record when you first met them, and where. Or why they were interested in what you sell. Whether or not you gave them a quote. When you were last in touch. Details on their business and product lines. The names of their spouse and children.

No problem. Computer databases allow you to do that. Okay, so let's add a few more things that may be useful. A calendar of key dates, for example. Your next appointment to call or see a client. The date of the client's big trade show or conference. Maybe even their birthday or anniversary. Again, no problem.

In what form would this information be most useful to you? Would you like to be able to sort your customers by telephone area code or by postal code? By their type of business or by the kind of product you sell to them? Would it be useful if you were given daily or weekly reminders of whom you need to contact?

With the right database, you can do all of that, and much more. Current database programs are designed to help you store whatever information you want, retrieve it easily, and make mailing to or contacting your VIPs (very important prospects) easier than ever before.

TYPES OF INFORMATION YOU SHOULD HAVE ON YOUR DATABASE

CONTACT INFORMATION

This is the type of information you might find in a business-card file or Rolodex:

- contact name
- title
- company name
- mailing address
- address for courier deliveries
- phone and fax numbers (including mobile and residence numbers)
- e-mail address
- web site

ACTION REMINDER

Your database should include space where you can record the next time and date to call, meet, or mail something to a prospect or client. This is sometimes referred to as an action, reminder, tickler, or bring-forward file.

PERSONAL INFORMATION

You may have reason to record each contact's birthday, anniversary, special dates, family members, alma mater, hobbies, sports, special interests, family background, religion, special awards, degrees, favourite vacation, etc.

HISTORY/LOG OF CONTACTS

You will also want to keep track of all the contacts you have made with each person in your database: material sent, calls made, meetings held, service provided, invoices sent and paid.

NOTES

Your database should include a free-form area for notes — what you discussed with the prospects, what is important to them, how you feel about them, details of quotes or agreements, who referred you to them, directions to their location.

CATEGORIES

All prospects are not equal. And some are on your database for different reasons. The more you can segregate your lists, the more specific you can be in the way you treat and contact them. And that leads to more efficient use of your time and money. If you use your resources and marketing efficiently, your sales will grow.

Choose database categories that make sense to you and your business. For example, you might categorize entries by the relationship you have with them: regular client, past client, prospect, supplier. Or you might segregate your database according to what groups the contacts belong to: chamber member, member of association A, member of association B, alumnus of your school.

SOME CATEGORY TERMS AND DEFINITIONS:

Clients	bought from you
Prospects	might buy from you
Supporters	will recommend you if asked
Advocates	will rave about you without being asked
Influencers	have the power to influence prospects or media
Associates	might collaborate with you on a project
Brain Trust	are supportive colleagues with whom you trade ideas and advice
Top 25	are the twenty-five people who must never lose sight of you
Lunch 100	comprises the 100 people you want to have lunch with this year

---

It might be useful to categorize by the type of business the contacts are in: manufacturing, service, import/export, retail. Or you could break them down by special interests: golfers, community volunteers, theatre-goers.

Categories allow you to search quickly for groups of names that have one or more of these dimensions in common. When you are planning your marketing activities, you can look at all these factors to see what elements your prospects have in common, or to discover opportunities for new markets.

Category searches should give you instant results. If you must wait several minutes or even seconds for the results of your search, that is too long.

It's also a good idea to create more than one database file. One would be your main customer and prospect file. Another might be for members of your association or service club. Another for classmates. Another for competitors. And yet another for those who attended your seminars or speeches — if you use speeches to promote your business.

Other categories you might use (use these or create your own):

- AAA = hot prospect
- AA = no current needs but they like me
- A = key influencer
- media
- CEO
- member of your club

5.2 BUILDING YOUR DATABASE

Where do you get new names? You can begin by adding every worthwhile *business card* you collect. Remember, some are a waste of time (e.g., those that you put in your left pocket). But include anyone who might be able to use your services or can influence others who might use your services.

Remember to collect cards at prospect meetings, networking sessions, association meetings, special events, seminars, trade shows, volunteer functions, even on airplanes when you strike up a conversation with someone interesting.

You will also get contact names from *referrals* (a colleague says, "You should call so and so"); from your *cold calls* (more on making cold calls later in this chapter); from *announcements* in the papers (you see a notice of a promotion or new position and send a note of congratulations); from *people in the news* (you read about a potential client or influencer in a newspaper or magazine).

Other good sources of names are *directories* for associations, chambers of commerce, municipal business listings, and club memberships. Often a printed version is free with membership. Some are online and many are available on CD. You can buy these directories or visit your public library.

Collect names by *offering free information*. You can make these offers on your web site, by e-mail, with a short note at the end of your published articles, or in an ad. When the requests come in, send the information and add the addresses to your database.

Trade names with another business. You could *exchange databases* with another company that sells to the same market that you do.

Rent or buy names from a *mailing list company*. Companies that compile, rent, and sell mailing lists are handy when you need to do a special mailing. Their lists can be very specific to your demographic needs.

Read the *job ads* — especially the management and executive listings. If you sell to engineers, notice any listings for managers of engineers. Note in your database file to call two months after the ad appeared. When you call, get the name of the new manager and send a congratulatory note, then follow up two weeks later to set a meeting. New people are often looking to make a change, and may be considering new suppliers.

5.3 USING COLD CALLS TO MAKE CONTACTS

Brrrrr — why do they call them "cold" calls? Because the thought of making them sends chills through even the bravest of souls. You might be able to talk on the phone for hours with a friend. But imagine calling someone who doesn't know you from Adam or Eve. You have to explain who you are and why the heck you are calling. You are so afraid you might sound like one of those people who call you at home in the evenings asking to clean your ducts or pave your driveway. The person at the other end of the line might hang up at any second, so you blurt it out and pray. You feel at their mercy.

And what if you are prevented from reaching your cold contact by the dreaded "gatekeeper"?

No problem. Believe in yourself, read the tips below, then start dialling.

SOME TIPS ON MAKING COLD CALLS
BEFORE YOU START
Have the list of names and numbers ready. No skipping names once you start. Spend time preparing your list before you start calling. You may grow less willing to continue after you get turned down a few times.

Have everything you need ready before you start, script notes, pricing, calendar, pen, and pad. And visit the bathroom beforehand; you want no distractions.

Get yourself "in the mood." Drink water, rehearse your script, think positively. Stretch, then sit or stand tall and confidently. Remind yourself how much that last customer loved your service.

Be clear on why you are calling. Your purpose might be to book a meeting, to discover the contact's short- or long-term needs, to get additional contact names, to introduce yourself, to learn their criteria for good service, to discover what suppliers they use now — or some combination of these goals.

> Fear defeats more people
> than any other one thing in the world.
> — *RALPH WALDO EMERSON*

WHOM SHOULD YOU CALL?
Always start as high in the organization as you can. It is better to be referred down by the president than to fight uphill. If senior management

likes you and has a need for your product, they will arrange the paperwork and give the needed approval.

- First choice: CEO, president
- Second choice: VPs, general manager, senior executives

Just because you are selling don't assume that you should call the "buying department." Its official name may be Purchasing, Human Resources, or Administration, but really it is the Sales Prevention Department. Avoid it if possible.

The role of these departments is to say no. They are good at screening calls. They are trained to protect and follow a process. They tell others what they cannot do. You should only call them if you are selling a commodity that can save them pennies. That will make them look good to their managers.

The higher the value of the service you sell, the higher up in the organization you must go to make the deal. By the way, most CEOs don't get many cold calls, because salespeople believe that they can't or shouldn't cold call them. The fact is that with today's more accessible style of leadership, it is much easier to get to the CEO than it was years ago. Some CEOs even pride themselves on answering their own phones and returning all their calls. So when you call the CEO you are already standing out from the crowd. You must come across well. There is no doubt the risk is greater — if you mess up with the CEO, you are out on your butt. But if the CEO likes you, that can be very good for business.

When you talk to CEOs, understand that they got to where they are because they are good listeners. They will listen if you speak their language. They understand the big picture concepts, so don't drown them with details. If you want to know what CEOs hope for or stay awake worrying about, why not conduct a survey before you do your cold calling? Read more about surveys in Chapter 1 on Perceptions.

MAKING THE CALLS

Schedule a time every day when you will make cold calls. *Don't do anything else* during that time period. When one call is finished, dial the next.

Using a headset makes it easier to talk, and you don't suffer a pain in the neck from cradling the phone under your chin. At the end of the scheduled time period, stop. Better to stop fresh than beat. That way you'll think, "Wow, that wasn't so bad. Can't wait for next time."

Set goals (e.g., number of calls) and measure what you do. How many is enough will depend on your market and success rate. Your target might be anywhere from five to 100 calls a day. If you can make five to twenty calls in half an hour, then 100 calls a day is certainly possible — if you want to allot that much time to cold calling each day.

Sometimes you will reach the contact's voice mail, which is great. Then you can leave your rehearsed 30-second message — without interruption. Remember, leave your phone number twice — once at the start and once at the end of your message.

Very often you reach a gatekeeper. Get them on your side. Don't try to get past them. They will feel it in your voice. Instead, *ask for their help*.

Here's a tip: Gatekeepers feel protective of their charge. They want to feel valued and important. If you make them feel that way you will get cooperation instead of ice.

Sometimes you will actually reach the person you want. That is really great. Talk to them. Listen attentively and make notes: Do they sound interested, ambivalent, not interested? Should you call back or send information?

After each call, make a quick mental check. Is there anything you should have done differently?

When you speak to an individual, ask when you should call next. Whether they say to call in a few weeks, a few months, or never, record it in your database and follow up (or not) accordingly. The next time you call you can say, "Hi, I'm calling you back as you requested."

Cold calling is an activity that many people hate. But it works. Don't worry if you don't feel good — you may even feel sick just thinking about it. This is one thing that is worth doing imperfectly and improving. Just start, and keep at it. For more help on making cold calls, read *How to Make Hot Cold Calls*, by Steven J. Schwartz.

> Successful people do often the things
> that failures hate and avoid doing.

> I did it the same way I learned to skate
> — by doggedly making a fool of myself until I got used to it.
> — *George Bernard Shaw, on how he became such a*
> *compelling speaker*

5.4 MAINTAINING YOUR DATABASE

Every time you make a call, receive a call, send or receive mail, or have meeting, record it in your database.

Open your database every day. Check your daily action reminders, and act on them.

For your computer database to work efficiently, you'll need to use the program functions to re-index and compress it periodically. These are software functions that you should learn to use right from the beginning.

Purge the database regularly. When contacts do not pan out, delete their records and move them to an archive file if necessary.

BACKING UP YOUR DATABASE
Every computer will mess up on you sooner or later. Back up.

1. *First-thing backup* — At the beginning of each day, make a copy of your database by saving it on your hard drive under a different name (e.g., save your "Client" database as "ClientA"). If something goes wrong, you won't lose the whole database — just the work that had been done that day. If you're making a great deal of changes in a day, you may wish to make backup copies more frequently. It only takes a few seconds, but it could save you hours of anguish.
2. *Daily backup* — Every day, create a backup to diskette, tape, CD, or cartridge. Have two sets of backups; one for odd days and one for even days. That way if there is a bug in your system you have backups from at least two different days. You may wish to back up data files to diskette and do a general backup to cartridge.

3. *Weekly backup* — Do a general backup that you keep offsite. It's a good idea to keep several copies and at least two sets — one for every other week. You might store the copies with your neighbour, your friends, or in a safety deposit box. If there is a fire or break-in at your office you can still carry on your business. Some people even back up their data to a secure area of their web site.

> You never appreciate backups until you need them.
> So back up or prepare to kick yourself.

5.5 LEVERAGING YOUR DATABASE

I HAVE TO ADMIT . . .

I'm no computer whiz or database expert. The reason I learned so much about database marketing was by accident on one of my projects.

Many years ago, I did some work for a Chamber of Commerce. They invited me to speak at one of their meetings, and said they would be doing a promotional mailing for it. So I asked them if they would be willing to send flyers to my prospects as well. To my surprise, they said yes.

I told them I had about 350 names on my list; I didn't at the time, but I knew I'd find them somewhere, even if I had to include my mother-in-law. They then gave me 350 of their envelopes, and I hired someone to type my addresses on them. (This was either before the age of labels, or before I could afford them.) The Chamber then stuffed, stamped, and mailed them for me. "Wow," I thought. "What a great way to market. Get somebody else to do most of it for you!"

That was just the beginning. I started to collect all the names I could of people who might be interested in my services. I asked each organization that hired me if they would consider a mailing to their members and my prospects (knowing that if I could put more people in the organizations' meetings, everyone would benefit).

On another occasion, I presented a speech to Arctic College, way up north in Yellowknife. My book *Secrets of Power Presentation* is required reading there (but not only there). They wrote two letters of referral for me — one to other colleges and universities, the other to 2,500 of my prospects across Canada. The opening read "Dear Friends Down South." They were excellent, supportive letters, and got us both a lot of attention! (By the way, with a mailing of that size I did help them cover costs, but it was worth it.)

I've now done piggyback-type mailings through many top companies, Boards of Trade, conferences and trade shows, business seminars, and more.

The point of this story is this: If it worked for me, it will work for you. All you have to do is ask — and have your mailing list or database ready.

— *PETER*

THE BENEFITS OF PIGGYBACKING

If you get others to talk about you, then arrange for them to send mail to your clients, just imagine how your customers will begin to view you. This month, they get a mailing from the Board of Trade about an upcoming event — and they see you're one of the speakers. Next month, they receive a conference program in the mail, and — that's right — your name is featured prominently. You don't have to be a professional speaker; it can work for many different products and services. (It also helps if you *do* speak to groups about your business. It's great exposure, and those groups can market you too.)

When someone else mails out for you, the impact is greater than if you do it yourself. No longer is the mailing just you telling prospects how great you are and why they're crazy if they don't buy your product. Instead, it's some other business or organization telling their own members or prospects that they should listen to you. It brings you added credibility. It increases your exposure. It gets others talking about you. And it reduces your direct mailing costs — and your workload.

My database now contains well over 10,000 names. In the software program I use, ACT!, I have names coded for three levels of top prospects: hot, hot-hot, and too hot to forget! They are divided into about forty different groups, by industry, association, colleges and universities, media, and the like. I can mail out to just one group or to them all. I also include important client information, which I update every time I speak or mail to them. For example, I like to know about big events in my clients' lives — weddings, bar mitzvahs, and so forth. These are important days to them, and it gives us something fun to talk about. Remember, marketing is not only about your products and services; it's about relationships.

I also make notes on the prices I've quoted for my books and speeches, delivery dates, bookings and future contacts, e-mail, fax and phone information, when I last sent them a Swiss chocolate bar, all of that — and it's all in the same database file. (See what I mean? It's far more than an address book, but just as easy to use.)

When I do an event in Calgary, Montreal, or wherever, I will often send (via e-mail) my list of contacts in that city/region to the event organizer there. "Why don't you send a mailing to these people?" I suggest. "It will bring in more people and get you more media exposure." Not a bad way to help a client, is it? You could do the same with your clients, associates, distributors, or whomever else you are working with when you are away from your office.

Without exaggeration, my database is the best way I have of staying in touch with those individuals who bring me a living and are interested in my work. I use it as often as possible. To send postcard updates on what I'm doing. For brochures on charity events I organize, for press releases, for mailings by my clients, for . . . well, you get the picture. It is an indispensable tool in my marketing.
— PETER

DON'T HAVE A PRODUCT TO SELL?

Database marketing — or mailing regularly to clients and prospects — can work in almost any field. Big companies know this (have you looked at your mail lately?). Small ones don't think they can compete, but they can.

Imagine you're a consultant. You could send out information on your current projects, new trends in the field, or articles of interest to clients. You're an entrepreneur? Great. No one knows what that is, anyway, so you can send anything of interest to prospects and they'll remember you: new product developments, new services, or notices of big new orders.

Make sure the information is useful *and* interesting. Use something prospects might want to post on their walls. Don't send just anything. It has to have thought, caring, and quality behind it. There is so much stuff out there that yours will get filed under G for Garbage (or R for Recycling) if you don't give them something good.

WHOM WILL CLIENTS SELECT?

When faced with a buying decision, whom do clients generally select? Experience and observation show this: Many do not select the *best* product or service supplier out there. They select the *last* — that is, the last one that came through their office or across their desk.

Think about it. When you need something, how often do you go to your files and sort through the reams of paper that people have sent you over the years, trying to find the perfect supplier? Sounds pretty unlikely. Most of us would go through our mental database instead and pull out — what? The last person we remember. That person may not always get the job, but at least they'll get invited to submit a quote, estimate, or proposal.

Salespeople know this principle well. It's called "last in." Often they will get business simply because they showed up at the customer's door.

You may not see yourself as a salesperson. And you don't have to. Just show up in your clients' in-baskets regularly, and you will see the results. Test this principle and see for yourself.

THE STONE CUTTER

He will hammer away at a rock 100 times without a crack showing in it. Then at the 101st blow it will split in two. It is not that blow alone that accomplished the result, but the 100 others that went before as well.

— *AUTHOR UNKNOWN*

SUMMARY
SECRETS OF DATABASE MARKETING

- Collect information about your clients and prospects that may help you market and sell to them. Use categories to track and find common groups.
- Protect your database. Back up often and plan for Murphy to visit your computer.
- Schedule your cold calls and your follow-up calls at separate times and stick to your schedule.
- Leverage your database by sharing and trading lists, and by getting other companies to mail to your list.
- Start high when you're approaching a new prospect company — contact the CEO or president. At each important company, stay in touch with more than one contact.

Final Words

This book is not about creating complicated marketing plans. It is meant to be read — not to awe or intimidate you.

> Why don't you write books people can read?
> — *NORA JOYCE TO HER HUSBAND, JAMES*

We attempted to write the book using simple but powerful words and ideas. Most of the ideas come from our own collection of strategies, techniques, and tips. Read them, think about them, and act.

> Education is an admirable thing,
> but it is well to remember from time to time
> that nothing that is worth knowing can be taught.
> — *OSCAR WILDE*

We assure you that along the way everyone makes mistakes — we did. But that should never be cause for quitting, or for failing to begin.

> Never let the fear of striking out get in your way.
> — *BABE RUTH*

If you are a new entrepreneur, congratulations! Welcome to an exciting world of self-determination.

> There is nothing in a caterpillar
> that tells you it's going to be a butterfly.
> — *BUCKMINSTER FULLER*

This book can open a wealth of opportunities for you.

> Opportunity is missed by most people
> because it is dressed in overalls and looks like work.
> — *THOMAS EDISON*

Most importantly . . .

> It's not the number of ideas you have,
> it's how many you put into action!
> *Go do it!*

Appendix A
101 Power Marketing Ideas

Use this page to brainstorm on the ideas you have learned from this book. Circle words at random. Put ideas together. Twist others. Maximize your Power Marketing potential. You may wish to photocopy this page, then scribble all over it. Have fun exploring the possibilities — they're endless!

adapt	friends	notes	service
advice	good news	number one	signs
articles	hobbies	obstacles	slogan
association	humour	partner	speak
award	image	pay for service	special events
bad news	information	perception	special skills
barter	Internet	photograph	sponsor
books	licensing	piggyback	staff
business cards	listen	positioning	strengths
coffee	logo	post cards	substitute
colour	luck	presentations	survey
combine	lunch	pricing	tapes
complaints	magazine	promise	technology
computers	maximize	prospects	testimonials
confidence	media	purpose	thank you
contests	mentor	put to another use	30 seconds
creativity	minimize	quality	time
culture	modify	questions	TV
customers	money	radio	value
emotion	name	referrals	vision
erase	negotiate	reverse	voice mail
family	networking	risk	volunteer
fax	newspapers	rules	weaknesses
finder's fee	niche	seasonal news	web site
flexibility	no charge	seminars	write
			zig zag

Appendix B
References

••

Career Growth

Bridges, William. *Job Shift: How to Prosper in a Workplace Without Jobs.* Reading, Massachusetts: Addison-Wesley, 1994.

Communication Skills

Bender, Peter Urs. *Secrets of Power Presentations.* Toronto: TAG, 1997.

Frank, Milo O. *How to Get Your Point Across in 30 Seconds or Less.* New York: Pocket Books, 1986.

Creativity

Basadur, Min. *Simplex: A Flight to Creativity.* Buffalo: Creative Education Foundation Press, 1994.

Michalko, Michael. *Thinkertoys.* Berkeley, CA: Ten Speed Press, 1991.

Osborn, Alex F. *Applied Imagination.* Buffalo: Creative Education Foundation Press, 1993.

von Oech, Roger. *A Kick in the Seat of the Pants.* Toronto: Harper Collins, 1986.

von Oech, Roger. *A Whack on the Side of the Head.* New York: Warner Books, 1990.

Directories

Canadian Trade Index (an index of over 25,000 Canadian manufacturers). www.ctidirectory.com
  (416) 798-8000

Sources (a listing of "experts" for the media).
  (416) 964-7799 Fax: (416) 964-8763

Who's Who in Canada. Markham, ON: International Press Publications.
  (905) 946-9588 Fax: (905) 946-9590

Who's Who of Canadian Women. Toronto: Maclean Hunter.
(416) 596-5156 Fax: (416) 596-5235

General Business

Beck, Nuala. *Shifting Gears: Thriving in the New Economy.* Toronto: HarperPerennial, 1993.

Cohon, George. *To Russia with Fries.* Toronto: McClelland & Stewart, 1997.

Gross, Daniel (ed.). *Forbes Greatest Business Stories of All Time.* New York: John Wiley & Sons, 1996.

Mackay, Harvey. *Beware the Naked Man Who Offers You His Shirt.* New York: Morrow, 1990.

Mackay, Harvey. *Swim with the Sharks Without Being Eaten Alive.* New York: Morrow, 1988.

Spence, Rick. *Secrets of Success from Canada's Fastest Growing Companies.* Toronto: John Wiley & Sons, 1997.

General Reference

Colombo, John Robert (ed.). *Canadian Global Almanac.* Toronto: Macmillan Canada (updated annually).

Internet

Carroll, Jim, and Rick Broadhead. *Canadian Internet Handbook.* Toronto: Prentice Hall (updated annually).

Marketing

Crandall, Rick. *Marketing Your Services.* Chicago: Contemporary Books, 1996.

Kremer, John. *1001 Ways to Market Your Books.* Fairfield, IA: Open Horizons, 1998.

Ries, Al, and Jack Trout. *The 22 Immutable Laws of Marketing.* New York: HarperBusiness, 1993.

Ringer, Robert J. *Winning Through Intimidation.* Los Angeles: Fawcett Books, 1993. (A book about attitude and confidence)

Williams, Robin. *The Non-Designer's Design Book.* Berkeley, CA: PeachPit, 1994. (Contains tips on simple graphic design for printed material)

Media Relations

Ramacitti, David. *Do-it-Yourself Publicity*. New York: AMACOM, 1990.

Yudkin, Marcia. *6 Steps to Free Publicity*. New York: Plume/Penguin, 1994.

Networking

Mackay, Harvey. *Dig Your Well Before You're Thirsty*. New York: Doubleday, 1997.

Personal Growth

Bender, Peter Urs. *Leadership from Within*. Toronto: Stoddart, 1997.

Canfield, Jack. *The Aladdin Factor*. New York: Berkley Pub. Group, 1995.

Cathcart, Jim. *The Acorn Principle*. New York: St. Martin's Press, 1998.

Goleman, Daniel P. *Emotional Intelligence*. New York: Bantam, 1997.

Griesseman, B. Eugene. *The Achievement Factors*. San Marcus, CA: Avant Books, 1990.

Sales

Bly, Robert W. *Selling Your Services*. New York: Henry Holt, 1991.

Morgen, Sharon Drew. *Sales on the Line*. Portland: Metamorphous Press, 1993. (Tips on how to sell on the phone)

Schwartz, Steven J. *How to Make Hot Cold Calls*. Toronto: Stoddart, 1997.

Steele, Paul, John Murphy, and Richard Russill. *It's a Deal: A Practical Negotiation Handbook*. London: McGraw Hill, 1989.

Trainor, Norm. *The 8 Best Practices of High-Performing Salespeople*. Toronto: Highrise Books, 1998.

Seminars and Professional Speaking

Walters, Dottie, and Lilly Walters. *Speak and Grow Rich*. New Jersey: Prentice Hall, 1989.

Appendix C
Web Sites

● ●

Here are a few web sites that you might find useful in your marketing work.

Associations
Directory of Canadian Associations   www.canadainfo.com

Presentation Resources
Canadian Association of Professional Speakers   www.canadianspeakers.org
National Speakers Association   www.nsaspeaker.org
Presentations magazine   www.presentations.com
Toastmasters   www.toastmasters.org

Media
Canada News Wire (database of news releases)   www.newswire.ca
Expert Radio (Internet radio)   www.expertradio.com
Yearbooknews (search engine used by news media)   www.yearbooknews.com
iRADIO (more Internet radio)   www.iradio.com

Marketing
Guerrilla Marketing Online   www.gmarketing.com
Wilson Internet Services (references and links for online marketing and
    e-commerce)   www.wilsonweb.com

For more web sites, visit:
www.PeterUrsBender.com
www.Torok.com and
www.PowerMarketing.ca

Index of Quotations

Subject Index

Presentations and Products

Lively keynotes and seminars offered
by either Bender or Torok

- Power Marketing™
- Leadership from Within™
- Power Presentations™

BOOKS
- *Secrets of Power Marketing*
- *Leadership from Within*
- *Secrets of Power Presentations*

TAPES
- *Secrets of Power Marketing*
2-audiotape set
- *Secrets of Power Presentations*
4-audiotape set (includes a 56-page workbook)

For single orders of books and tapes
call toll-free: 1-800-668-9372

Videotape program also available

Peter Urs Bender
The Achievement Group
108–150 Palmdale Drive
Toronto, ON, Canada M1T 3M7
(416) 491-6690 Fax: (416) 490-0375
www.PeterUrsBender.com

George Torok
The Knowledge Navigators
3211 Maderna Road
Burlington, ON, Canada L7M 2V6
(905) 335-1997 Fax: (905) 335-2176
www.Torok.com

Send your marketing tips and examples to SPM Hot Tips, c/o G. Torok.
You will receive a free copy of the latest SPM Hot Tips.
We may include your tips in the next book. Visit our web sites
to see more tips or to get your free subscription to the e-mail newsletters
Power Marketing™ and *Power Presentations*™.